Cranford

by Martyn Coleman

From the novel by

Mrs. Gaskell

WWW.SAMUELFRENCH.CO.UK
WWW.SAMUELFRENCH.COM

Copyright © 1951 Martyn Coleman
Reprinted 1956
All Rights Reserved

CRANFORD is fully protected under the copyright laws of the British Commonwealth, including Canada, the United States of America, and all other countries of the Copyright Union. All rights, including professional and amateur stage productions, recitation, lecturing, public reading, motion picture, radio broadcasting, television and the rights of translation into foreign languages are strictly reserved.

ISBN 978-0-573-11110-5

www.samuelfrench.co.uk
www.samuelfrench.com

FOR AMATEUR PRODUCTION ENQUIRIES

UNITED KINGDOM AND WORLD EXCLUDING NORTH AMERICA

plays@SamuelFrench-London.co.uk

020 7255 4302/01

Each title is subject to availability from Samuel French, depending upon country of performance.

CAUTION: Professional and amateur producers are hereby warned that CRANFORD is subject to a licensing fee. Publication of this play does not imply availability for performance. Both amateurs and professionals considering a production are strongly advised to apply to the appropriate agent before starting rehearsals, advertising, or booking a theatre. A licensing fee must be paid whether the title is presented for charity or gain and whether or not admission is charged.

The professional rights in this play are controlled by Samuel French Ltd, 52 Fitzroy Street, London, W1T 5JR

No one shall make any changes in this title for the purpose of production. No part of this book may be reproduced, stored in a retrieval system, or transmitted in any form, by any means, now known or yet to be invented, including mechanical, electronic, photocopying, recording, videotaping, or otherwise, without the prior written permission of the publisher. No one shall upload this title, or part of this title, to any social media websites.

The right of Martyn Coleman to be identified as author of this work has been asserted in accordance with Section 77 of the Copyright, Designs and Patents Act 1988.

Cranford

This play was first presented by the Derek Salberg and Basil Thomas Wolverhampton Repertory Company, under the direction of Basil Thomas, at the Grand Theatre, Wolverhampton, on 18 June, 1951, with the following cast:—

(In the order of their appearance)

Mrs. Gaskell	Sally Rogers
Miss Matilda Jenkyns (Miss Matty)	Dorothy Clement
Martha	Kathleen Rayner
Mary Smith	Judith Cuff
Miss Pole	Patricia Tucker
Miss Barker	Aimee Delamain
Mrs. Forrester	Betty Bowden
The Hon. Mrs. Jamieson	Peggy Mount
Mr. Hoggins	Gerald Cuff
Lady Glenmire	Ruth Perkins
Jem Hearn	Anthony Sagar

Directed by John Sykes

Décor by Pamela Lewis

The play takes place in the parlour of Miss Matty's house in the village of Cranford.

ACT ONE
Scene i. Noon on a sunny day in the late autumn of 1830.
Scene ii. Late afternoon of the following day.

ACT TWO
Scene i. Late afternoon, some months later.
Scene ii. About eight o'clock of an evening a week or so later.

ACT THREE
A bright sunny morning, two day's later
and
some months later. A bright summer morning.

PRODUCER'S NOTE

At the opening of each of the three Acts of this charming adaptation, Mrs. Gaskell herself appears as, so to speak, a 'chorus', to introduce the people of her novel, and to describe the scene of the village of Cranford. Her appearance is not essential, and the author is content to leave it to producers whether or not to omit her—as they will see, the play proceeds easily without her three introductions—but most will probably feel that she adds to the charm and cosiness of the piece.

In the original production, 'Cranford' was played in a frame: that is, a false prescenium arch was painted as a picture frame. This, again, is not a necessity, but it can be an attractive embellishment.

If producers decide to retain the introductory appearances of Mrs. Gaskell, they can be easily stage-managed. In the original production, Mrs. Gaskell entered from the wings down stage left, before a gauze curtain, in a small pool of light. As she speaks of her memories, the lights go up behind the gauze, the action synchronizes with the dialogue, and the feeling of happy reminiscence is created. If a gauze curtain presents any difficulty, much of the same effect can be obtained by simply spotlighting Mrs. Gaskell down-stage, and bringing up the stage lights behind her as the characters of the play appear. On each of Mrs. Gaskell's exits, of course, the gauze (if used) rises out of sight, and the down-stage spotlight fades out.

For general atmosphere, as the Ladies of Cranford are always bustling in breathlessly with tit-bits of news and scandal, speed is vital. This must be achieved without destroying the leisurely atmosphere of the period, but any danger of the action becoming static must be avoided.

Miss Matty's shop in Act III (set during a black-out) should be very simple. A swinging sign with "Miss Jenkyns' Tea Shop" attached to the wall, and a counter (pre-set) carried in complete with tea canisters, wrapping, etc., are almost all that is necessary (see plot). In this un-elaborate way, it appears that Miss Matty has made only a pathetic attempt to turn her house into a shop.

The lighting can be very charming and candles should be used for the practical stage lighting. In the original production, two large six-candle silver candelabra were used, and two single silver candlesticks. Apart from the spot, or spots, used for Mrs. Gaskell, the lighting was in two sections, i.e. enough to light the stage behind the gauze (when floodlights, etc. were useless) and the general lighting that faded in when the gauze curtain flew away. At the opening of the second Act, during Mrs. Gaskell's speech, the lights fade in behind the gauze and it is evening, i.e. some candles should be alight and the curtains drawn. It is impossible to have any light behind the gauze at the opening; therefore, Martha should be discovered on the stage to light the candles at the given cue and the stage lighting can fade in immediately afterwards. The same principle would apply if no gauze curtain were used.

The costuming is reasonably simple, for the Ladies of Cranford have only two frocks. However, care should be given to Miss Pole as the eccentricities of her character can best be expressed in her clothes rather than broadening the performance with the subsequent danger of 'coming out' of the picture.

To keep the play in its frame—a picture of charm and memories—is the real essence.

LIONEL HALE

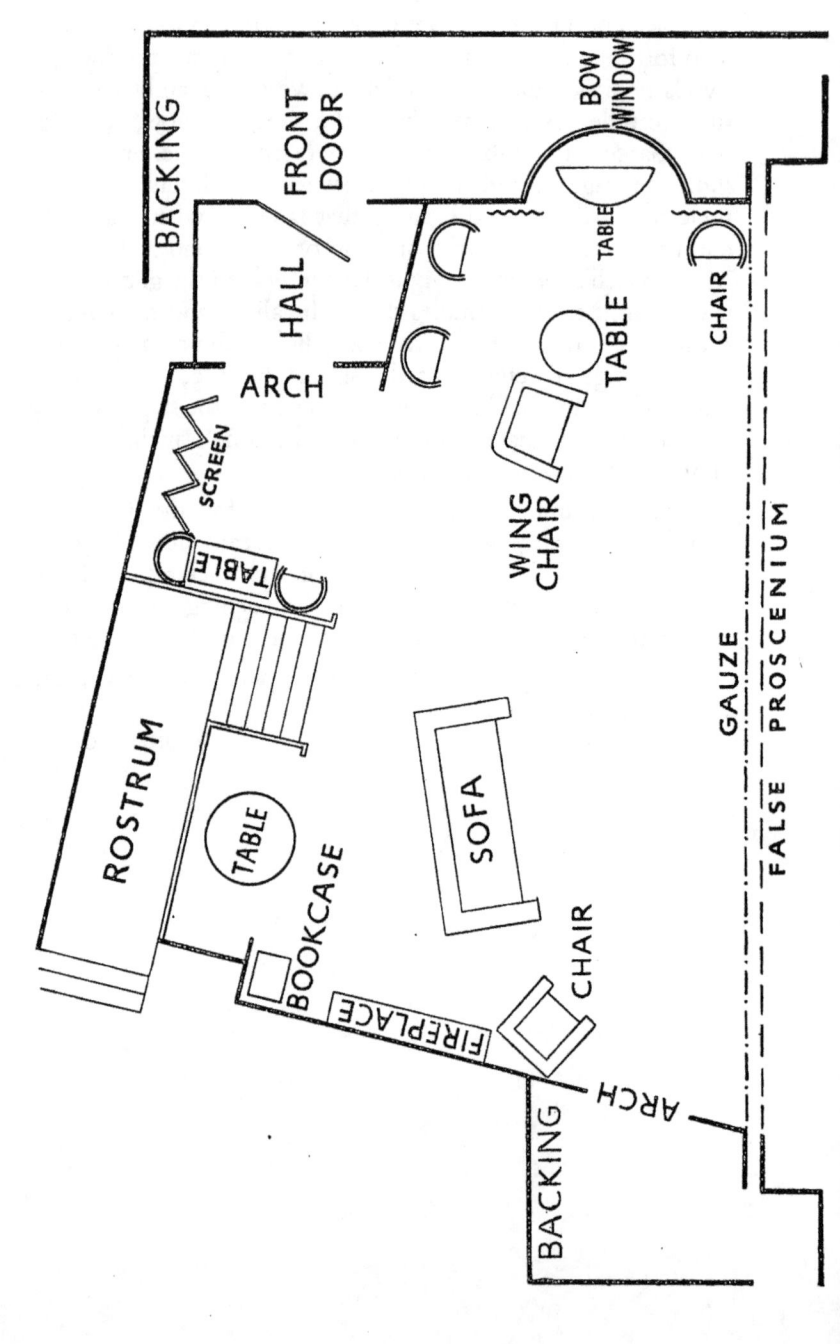

CRANFORD MISS MATTY'S PARLOUR (Courtesy—Grand Theatre, Wolverhampton.)

CHARACTERS

Mrs. Gaskell
Miss Matilda Jenkyns (Miss Matty)
Martha
Mary Smith
Miss Pole
Miss Barker
Mrs. Forrester
The Hon. Mrs. Jamieson
Mr. Hoggins
Lady Glenmire
Jem Hearn

CRANFORD

ACT ONE

SCENE I

The entire action of the play takes place in MISS MATTY'S parlour in the village of Cranford.

TIME: About noon on a sunny day in the late Autumn of the year 1830.

To all intents and purposes the set is triangular, the longest side running from U.S.R. to D.S.L. and terminating in a small bay window which commands a view of the front door and path. The archway containing this window is heavily curtained.

The upstage wall contains a large recess which accommodates, U.R., a small landing and a short flight of stairs leading to it. Left of the stairs, the recess has a curtained exit, ostensibly the short passage leading to the front door.

In the centre of the other wall (stage R.) is a fireplace and D.R. a curtained archway leading to the kitchen and back stairs.

The furniture is of the period and consists of a sofa near the fireplace, which is also typical, an armchair D.R. between it and the archway, and a revolving book rack U.R. against the same wall. U.C. there is a screen, near the passage to the front door, also a small round table and two upright chairs. D.L. centre is another, and cosier, armchair with an occasional table beside it. In the small bay window is a table (or desk) on which is a candelabrum and other bric-à-brac. The heavily-papered walls should be well covered with portraits and miniatures in gilt frames and a bell-pull hangs beside, and below, the fireplace. The floor is carpeted, with a rug in front of the fireplace, which must contain an assortment of heavy fire-irons. There is a palm U.R. in the crook of the stairs and a vase of flowers is seen on the landing table. An atmosphere of prim respectability and limited resources pervades the scene.

ON CURTAIN rise enter from DOWN LEFT a lady, MRS. GASKELL, dressed in the style of about 1860 . . . She is middle-aged, comfortable, kindly . . . and her face denotes a character *in which humour and wisdom are pleasantly blended. She curtseys to the audience and commences to speak in the tone of one about to share a secret.*

MRS. GASKELL. My name is Gaskell... Mrs. Gaskell... and I am here to introduce you to Cranford... and to the society of Cranford... this is made up almost entirely of ladies. All these ladies are such dear friends of mine that I feel rather protective about them, almost motherly, and indeed I had always the same feelings toward them when I was quite a girl, nearly thirty years ago. Most of the ladies of Cranford were poor... at least only one of them was what might be termed rich... And, after all, what did riches signify?... because any exhibition whatever of wealth was considered vulgar... But in those days, when I visited Cranford so frequently, a revolution took place. A very genteel revolution yes... even in those days progress was on the march; though perhaps one might say that in Cranford progress marched upon tip-toe! I lived at that time with my family in Drumble, and I used frequently to visit Miss Matilda Jenkyns, an old friend of my father.

(As MRS. GASKELL *speaks the lights slowly fade in behind the gauze cloth revealing a room neat and fresh looking. The only thing at all remarkable about it is that across the floor in a direct line from the window lie a series of newspapers. They are there to shield the carpet from the injurious rays of the sun, and, if we are slightly puzzled at first as to their purpose, we shall very soon discover it.)*

Now this is the occasion of one of my many visits; I remember I came in response to an appealing note from Miss Matty who found herself faced with the fearful problem of breaking in a new maid. But I came eagerly for Cranford was always to me a place of great events and great excitements, and Miss Matty made much of me... But here is Miss Matty herself.

(Enter MISS MATTY, *door* U.L. *She is a pretty, delicate woman, in her forties... but dressed with precision, almost primness... and wearing the inevitable lace cap.)*

ACT 1, SCENE 1] CRANFORD 11

We see she has a small bunch of chrysanthemums in her hand. She crosses the stage, takes a glass vase from a shelf . . . and goes out to kitchen.)

MRS. G. See . . . she has gathered some late flowers . . . they are to put in my room, I'm sure . . . I am due to arrive any minute now.

(Enter from kitchen, D.R., MARTHA . . . she is a servant . . . of the rough and ready type . . . a healthy country girl . . . . as yet unbroken. Her cap is askew . . . and her sleeves are rolled up showing brawny arms. She carries a silver tea-tray which she is polishing . . . breathing heavily upon it and rubbing it with the corner of her apron. She looks at it critically then places it under the sofa where it is hidden by the flounces.)

And this must be the new maid . . . I can see she certainly needs breaking in . . . that's right . . . the tray always lives under the sofa . . . No burglar would dream of looking for it there . . .

(As she is leaving the room MARTHA kicks aside one of the newspapers which lie across the floor. At this moment MISS MATTY enters again from the kitchen . . . she is about to mount the stairs with the flowers she has arranged in the vase when she sees the displaced newspaper. She sets down the flowers and positively runs to put it back in place.)

Gracious! In another moment the sun might have fallen directly upon the carpet . . . and it might in time have become faded . . .

(At this moment the DOORBELL rings . . . MARTHA and MISS MATTY become suddenly rigid . . .)

MRS. G. Oh, dear! Here I come . . . and too early by some minutes . . . Poor Miss Matty, and she has not yet changed her cap. In Cranford our old caps are worn always in the mornings, and hastily changed if a visitor should appear . . .

MISS MATTY *(in a flutter and fussing about her cap)*. Quickly, Martha . . . see who can be at the door . . .

(MARTHA proceeds to the front door as if to open it.)

My goodness! No . . . no . . . not the door . . .

Mrs. G. Of course not . . . The window first . . . it would never do to open the door without first inspecting the caller . . .

(Martha *has halted in her tracks . . . baffled.*)

Miss Matty. Always remember, Martha . . . the window first . . .

(Martha *proceeds to the window and is about to push aside the lace curtain . . .*)

Not the curtain . . . you will be seen. Just peep . . .

(Martha *peeps.*)

Who is it?

(Martha *returns stolidly centre as if about to continue with her work . . .*)

Who is it, Martha?

Martha (*casually*). A body.

Miss Matty. A body? You must not say "a body".

Martha. A respectable body.

Miss Matty. Oh dear . . . (Miss Matty *runs to the window herself*). Oh . . . it is Miss Mary, come already. (*She takes a deep breath . . . we can see she is determined to be practical at all costs.*) Now, Martha . . . take up these papers. I will take these flowers to Miss Mary's room and change my cap . . . when I am ready for you to open the door I will cough . . . like this . . . (*She gives a genteel cough.*)

Martha. Yes, m'am.

(Miss Matty *takes the flowers and scuttles up the stairs.* Martha *picks up the newspapers looking slightly bewildered.*)

Mrs. G. And lest you should feel any nervousness on account of the caller who is waiting on the step, I must tell you that this proceeding is the accepted thing in Cranford. The caller knows quite well what is going on inside the house and would not for the world ring a second time or give any other cause for embarrassment . . .

(Martha, *having collected the papers, goes to the window and examines the visitor with some interest.*)

And in this case, of course, it is I who am waiting on that doorstep . . . Martha seems to find me interesting . . . Indeed I am rather curious myself . . . I wonder how I

looked thirty years ago . . .
>   (MISS MATTY *appears on the lower steps of the stairs . . . tolerably composed, and gives the genteel cough. But* MARTHA *is too interested in the window and does not hear.* MISS MATTY *coughs again . . . rather louder . . . still no response.* MISS MATTY *crosses to a chair . . . seats herself, coughs again . . . and takes up a book.*)

MISS MATTY. I coughed, Martha . . .
>   (MARTHA *starts . . . and then tears to the front door with the bundle of papers still under her arm.*)

Martha . . . ! (*In a note of warning.*)
>   (*But* MARTHA *has wrenched open the door and stands back rather breathlessly and triumphantly.*
>   *Enter* MARY. *She is an attractive girl . . . quiet and unassuming; she walks into the hallway and looks expectantly around. She carries a hat-box.*)

MRS. G. Oh, dear . . . there I am . . . (*She sighs reminiscently.*) But you must remember this was thirty years ago.
>   (*Exit* MRS. G. LEFT. *The gauze rises.*
>   MARTHA *still stands helplessly. She has opened the door and can do no more, so* MARY *smiles at her and steps past her into the room.*)

MARY (*holding out her arms*). Miss Matty . . . !
MISS MATTY (*laying down her book*). Why, Mary . . . !
>   (*They embrace.*)

MARY. Miss Matty, my bag . . . I came in the station fly . . . the driver has the rheumatics and cannot carry it . . . Could . . . ? (*She turns towards* MARTHA.)
MISS MATTY. Martha! Miss Mary's bag . . . please bring it from the fly . . . Poor Matthew, he has the rheumatics again, and only last week I told his wife to place red flannel on his back . . . it is the surest cure . . .
>   (MARTHA *is still agape.*)

Quick, Martha! The bag . . . and tell Matthew . . . red flannel . . . Quickly, girl . . .
>   (MARTHA *comes to life . . . looks for somewhere to deposit the papers, thrusts them at* MARY, *and gallops from the room . . .*)

MISS MATTY. Oh dear... she is sadly clumsy... I am afraid I have no ability in the training of servants... My sister Deborah was so clever, she could take a raw country girl and train her so well...

MARY (*crossing in front of* MISS MATTY). Don't worry, Miss Matty... I expect I can talk to her and after a few weeks she will be quite different... But these papers, you should not have taken them up for me... (*She starts to lay them again on the strip of sunlight.*)

MISS MATTY. Oh... thank you, my dear...
(*They carefully arrange them together.*)
It was a very valuable carpet... some years ago, and I would not have it fade...
(*Enter* MARTHA *with bag... she slams the door behind her...*)
Oh...! You see she will always slam the door... Take Miss Mary's bag to her room, Martha...
(MARTHA *plunges towards the stairs.*)
Ah! Martha!... The back stairs, if you please.
(*Exit* MARTHA D.R. *to kitchen.*)
It saves wear on the stair carpet, you know...

MARY. She seems a willing girl... she will soon learn...

MISS MATTY (*sitting* L.C.). It was so kind of you to come, my dear... and so kind of your dear father to spare you... You are such a practical girl... and I am afraid I am not strong-minded enough to break in such a boisterous spirit...

MARY (*placing her hat box on sofa and sitting*). Don't worry, Miss Matty... just a little training...

MISS MATTY (*rather shyly*). And there are some things that are so difficult to mention... to a servant...

MARY. You leave it to me...

MISS MATTY. There is one thing in particular... you see...
(*She halts in confusion.*)

MARY. Yes...?

MISS MATTY. My sister Deborah, when she was alive, was most particular about it... and I believe it is very necessary... at least so I have been told... with young girls... of the servant classes, I mean, of course...

MARY. Yes, Miss Matty...?
MISS MATTY. Oh dear... Well, what I refer to is...' (*She lowers her voice.*) ... men...!
MARY. I'm sure Martha is a good, decent girl...
MISS MATTY. Oh, of course.... but I believe that among the lower classes it is not unusual to encourage followers... in the kitchen, you know...
MARY (*smiling*). I'll talk to her about it...
MISS MATTY (*much relieved*). Thank you, my dear... You see, as my sister used to say... Our father was the rector of Cranford and we must set an example... in all details of our household...
MARY. I shall not leave you until Martha is a model to every other maidservant in the town...
MISS MATTY. Thank you, Mary... then I shall leave everything in your hands... (*She rises.*) And now... let me take you to your room.
  (MARY *rises.* MARTHA *enters from* D.R.)
Ah... your hat-box...... Martha, Miss Mary's hat-box ... (*She suddenly remembers something.*) ... Oh, yes... the hat-box.... Did you... did you remember my little commission...?
MARY. Indeed I did... as if I could forget...! (*She is moving towards the stairs.*)
MISS MATTY (*rather shy again*). And is it... is it... in there? (*She indicates the hat-box.*)
MARY (*seeming in no hurry to exhibit the commission*). Yes... I have it quite safe... and it is very pretty too...
MISS MATTY (*with ill-concealed excitement*). Of course, there is no hurry... it is not of great importance.... but... (*She adds with a rush.*) I hear that they are quite the thing in London and I believe it will be the first to be seen in Cranford...
MARY (*a little nervous now, crossing behind sofa*). Miss Matty... I do not wish you to be disappointed...
MISS MATTY. Oh, I am sure I shall not be. You have such very good taste... such an elegant taste indeed... Perhaps we might just look at it...

MARY. You see ... what you described ... in your letter ...
MISS MATTY. Yes, yes ... I copied the description from the St. James's Chronicle ... it was written by a lady of quality it said ... an exact description of the new turban worn by Her Majesty, Queen Adelaide at Court ...
MARY (*embarrassed*). But, Miss Matty ... you are so pretty ... a turban is such a heavy, clumsy thing ...
MISS MATTY. Satin, it was ... and sea-green ...! (*She crosses to sofa.*) Perhaps we will just take a peep at it now ... Not, of course, that I care about dress ... but I would like to look tidy ... and having heard that Queen Adelaide herself ...

    (*She takes the hat-box and is about to open it when she sees that* MARTHA *has approached and is peering over her shoulder ...*)

Martha ...! The kitchen ...!
    (*Exit* MARTHA.)
MARY (*crossing below sofa*). Miss Matty ... before you open it ... I must tell you that I did not bring a turban ... They are such vastly ugly things and not suitable at all for Cranford ... had you but seen them you would agree ...
MISS MATTY (*terribly crestfallen*). Oh ... not a turban ...
MARY (*eagerly producing from the box a very pretty cap ... all lace and lavender ribbons*). But this cap—look ... how pretty it is ... And it will be so becoming, I know ...
MISS MATTY (*with resignation but no interest*). Perhaps you are right, my dear. I am sure you did your best. It is just like the caps all the ladies in Cranford are wearing, and they have had theirs for a year, I dare say ...
MARY (*twirling it round*). See ... both back and side-fronts ... and such pretty ribbons ...
MISS MATTY. It is very pretty, my dear. And, after all ...! What does it signify, what we wear here in Cranford, where everybody knows us!
MARY. Come ... try it on ...
MISS MATTY. Here? In the parlour?
MARY. No one will see ...
MISS MATTY (*removing and giving* MARY *the cap she is wearing*)

Miss Pole   Miss Matty   Mary   Miss Barker

Act Three. A corner of the parlour, in front of the bay window D.L., converted into Miss Matty's tea shop.

(*Courtesy–Grand Theatre, Wolverhampton.*)

Well ... since we are quite alone ... (*She takes the new cap.*) Now, this must be the back ... and this ...
   (*There is a violent peal on the doorbell.*
   At once they are both electrified and stand paralysed. Enter MARTHA ... *she makes for the front door.*)
MISS MATTY. Martha! ... No ... not the door ...
   (MARTHA *halts in her tracks and* MARY *goes to the window where she carefully inspects the caller* ... *Meanwhile* MISS MATTY *is feverishly collecting caps and tissue paper and preparing to escape up stairs.*)
MARY. It is only Miss Pole ...
MISS MATTY. Miss Pole? Oh ... but nonetheless ... Oh, dear ... and I am not even dressed ... !
MARY. But, Miss Pole ... we need not stand upon ceremony for her ...
MISS MATTY (*hesitates for a second, but tradition is too strong*). Dear Mary ..... I cannot appear without a cap. Now, Martha, ... wait for the cough.
   (*She proceeds upstairs but is not yet out of sight when we hear* MISS POLE *calling through the letterbox.*)
MISS POLE (*off ... and in excitement*). It is I ... Miss Pole ... I have news for you ... great news ... Miss Matty ... it is only I ... please do not bother to change your cap ...
MISS MATTY (*from stairs*). Oh, dear me ... How *did* she know?
   (*But she hurries off even faster.*)
MISS POLE (*still through the letterbox*). Please open the door, I beg of you ...
   (MARTHA *waits for no further orders but opens it and in dashes* MISS POLE. *Like all ladies of Cranford, she is over thirty-five ... bustling, vivacious and active. She guesses that* MISS MATTY *is upstairs and begins to mount the stairs at a good pace.*)
MARY. Miss Pole ... !
   (MISS P. *halts ... turns back into the room. Exit* MARTHA.)
MISS POLE (*embracing her warmly*). Why ... Mary! And how are you, my dear child, and how is your father? And did you have a safe journey ... those trains ... so dangerous I

declare ... I saw the station fly draw up here a while ago ... just happened to glance out of my window ... and I said to Betty "That will be Miss Mary, come to stay with Miss Matty, I dare say". For I knew you were coming today, of course ... on the railway ... though how your father can let you travel on the nasty, dangerous thing I don't know ...

(*She has removed her coat and hat, placing them on table* U.L.)

MARY. My father says the railway is a fine institution ...

MISS POLE. That may be ... but men are such gullible creatures ... they believe anything. I am told that the best means of travelling in safety on the things is to give the driver a shilling to go slow ...

MARY (*smiling*). My father has a friend who is a director of the railway and he assures me ...

MISS POLE (*crossing to sofa*). Pooh ... another man. They always wish to know everything and to be considered Samson and Solomon rolled into one ... Men have always foreseen events after they have happened ... though they never warn you beforehand ...

MARY. But, Miss Pole ...

MISS POLE (*crossing below sofa and in the manner of one giving the final proof to an argument*). Men ... ! Ugh ... ! I think I may claim to know the sex pretty well ... after all, my father was a man ... !

(MARY *is defeated ... and begins to loosen her cape and bonnet.* MISS POLE *sits.*)

Now ... where's Miss Matty?

(*At this moment the cough is heard on the stairs ... it is repeated.* MISS POLE *moves to* R. *of sofa and sits.*)

Don't bother to cough, Miss Matty ... I am already in ...

(*Enter* MISS M., *a little out of countenance.* MISS POLE *rises.*)

I know it is too early to call ... but I could not wait ... I have such news ...

MISS MATTY. How kind of you, Miss Pole. Will you not sit down, you are so out of breath? (MISS POLE *sits.*) And here is dear Mary come to stay with me again and help me with Martha ... is it not kind of her ... ?

MISS POLE (*impatient at being side-tracked*). Yes, yes, indeed, very kind and I have already greeted her and inquired after her father who is very well though he has rather unfortunate views about the railway ... But now ... what do you think ... ?

MISS MATTY (*crossing to* MARY, *quite genuinely distressed*). You must excuse me, Miss Pole ... But Mary is still wearing her cape and bonnet—how rude of me. What *can* I have been thinking about ... Martha!

(*Enter* MARTHA D.R.)

Here is Miss Mary's cape and bonnet ... take them to her room and lay them carefully on the bed ...

(*Exit* MARTHA. MISS MATTY *seats herself to* R. *of* MISS POLE ... *she adopts an expectant expression and waits for the news.*)

MISS POLE (*rising. She has waited for the audience*). Well, what do you think ... ? As I was just about to tell Mary, here, I had occasion to pop into Mr. Johnson's shop to match some ribbons ... and there was Miss Batty ...

MISS MATTY. Yes ... ?

MISS POLE. ... who had heard it straight ... well, almost straight, from Mr. Mulliner ...

MISS MATTY (*to* MARY). Mr. Mulliner is the Honourable Mrs. Jamieson's butler ...

MISS POLE. ... so it must be true.

MARY (*sitting on chair* L.C.). Dear Miss Pole, please tell us ...

MISS POLE (*after a suitable pause to increase the suspense*). Well ... yesterday ... by the noon train ... came a visitor to Cranford ... a guest of Mrs. Jamieson ... a lady ...

MISS MATTY (*eagerly*). Yes ... ? A lady ... ?

MISS POLE. Indeed, a lady ... in fact none other than the widow of the late Earl of Glenmire ... The Countess of Glenmire herself ... !

(*She stands back to savour her triumph ... which is indeed great, for both* MISS M. *and* MARY *are properly astonished.*)

MISS MATTY. The Countess of Glenmire ... !

MARY. Lady Glenmire ... !

Miss Matty. Have you seen her? What does she look like..?
Miss Pole (*rather vexed at being asked a question she cannot answer*). Look like...? Well... as to that... I didn't think to ask...
   (*At this moment* Martha *has descended the stairs again and has overheard the last words. She moves* D.R. *listening.*) But there is no doubt that Lady Glenmire would appear very distinguished...
Miss Matty. I have never seen a countess.
Martha (*unnoticed till now*). Is it the lady that's staying with Mrs. Jamieson, you mean...?
   (*They turn on her in unison.*)
Miss Matty. Oh... er, Martha...
Martha (*pausing with one hand on kitchen door*). Yes, m'am?...
Miss Matty. You understand I cannot encourage gossip about the ladies of Cranford... but I was just wondering if you happened to notice...
Martha. What, m'am?
Miss Pole. This lady with the Honourable Mrs. Jamieson, now... You saw her quite clearly...?
Martha. Clear enough.
Miss Matty. A very distinguished lady, no doubt...?
Martha. Put me in mind a bit of Mrs. Deacon, her at the Coach and Horses.
Miss Matty. Hush, Martha! That's not respectful.
Martha. Isn't it, m'am... I beg pardon.
   (*Exit* Martha. Miss Pole *sits on* L. *of* Miss M.)
Miss Pole (*exasperated*). I declare! The ignorance of the lower classes...!
Miss Matty. Well, I suppose we shall all see her sooner or later.
Miss Pole. Sooner or later! Tomorrow!
Miss Matty. Indeed? And does Mrs. Jamieson give a party?
Miss Pole. Not that I know of... but tomorrow is Thursday, is it not, and that is the day of your party...
Miss Matty. My party... Oh, my goodness! But I did not ask Lady Glenmire, I did not know she was here.
Mary. But do you give a party tomorrow, Miss Matty?

Miss Matty. Just a few friends, dear ... for tea and a game of preference ... Just the ladies of Cranford ... I thought it would be nice for them to welcome you ... and a little excitement for you to ...
Miss Pole. But you invited Mrs. Jamieson, did you not? And she accepted too?
Miss Matty. Dear me, yes ... but that was a week ago ...
Miss Pole. No matter ... Mrs. Jamieson is coming to the party, so, of course, she will bring Lady Glenmire ... she could hardly leave her alone ...
Miss Matty. Lady Glenmire! A countess ... ! Oh, dear ...
Mary. Now do not worry, Miss Matty ... we shall manage very well ... And with Martha to help ...
Miss Matty (*suddenly remembering* Martha). Martha ... ! Oh dear ... we must postpone the party ... it would not do at all ... with Martha not even broken ...
Miss Pole. I really think it would be considered very odd indeed to postpone it at the last moment ...
Miss Matty (*moaning*). Oh dear ... and Martha ...
Miss Pole. And, speaking as one of the ladies of Cranford, I should not wish Mrs. Jamieson to think we were frightened of her sister-in-law ... Mrs. Jamieson is such a very conceited woman and she might think we had never met a countess before—
Mary. And, after all, even a countess is only human ...
Miss Matty (*with relief*). Oh ... do you think so, my dear?
Miss Pole. And we will show Mrs. Jamieson that we are not at all impressed with her grand relations. I dare say she thinks we are not accustomed to deal with persons of title ...
Miss Matty. Well, I for one, must confess that I have never in my life met a countess ... or even a count for that matter.
Miss Pole (*rather taken aback*). Oh! (*But she rallies.*) But next to Mrs. Jamieson you are the social leader of Cranford ... the daughter of the ex-rector ... and everybody knows that you are related to Sir Peter and Lady Arley ...
Miss Matty. But Sir Peter and Lady Arley both died a long while ago and I'm sure I do not remember anything about

them...

MISS POLE (*anxiously*). But at least you remember how you addressed Lady Arley?

MISS MATTY (*still quite happy*). Oh no... in fact I cannot remember that I ever met Lady Arley... so you, Miss Pole, must coach us in the correct mode of addressing the peerage.

MISS POLE (*feeling very silly*). Well... you see... it is some time since I was in society... and I was wondering...

MISS MATTY. Dear Miss Pole... do you really not know...?

MISS POLE. It is just that I was wondering, do you say, *Your Ladyship* where you would say *You* to a common person... or is it only servants who say that...?

MISS MATTY. Servants...! Oh, Martha...!

MISS POLE. And then there's the matter of the curtsey...

MISS MATTY. I'm sure I shall not curtsey for I do not know how...

MISS POLE. I wonder if Mrs. Forrester would know... her father was in the army and fought against Napoleon...

MISS MATTY (*relieved again*). Then certainly she will know...

MISS POLE. I think I will just go and tell her about our little difficulty. I would not let Lady Glenmire think we were quite ignorant of the etiquettes of high life in Cranford...

MISS MATTY (*rising and moving to fireplace*). And will you just step in here, dear Miss Pole, as you come back, and tell us what you decide upon?

MISS POLE. And perhaps you wouldn't mind if I just glanced at the St. James's Chronicle... I would like just to catch up on the news from Court...

MISS MATTY. Of course... Mary, dear... the St. James's Chronicle, just by your elbow...

(MARY *hands it to* MISS POLE... *who starts to look through it.*)

We take it in turns, you know... first it goes to Mrs. Jamieson... then it comes to me... then I hand it on to Mr. Hoggins... and...

MISS POLE (*who has been thumbing through the pages*). Ah!... here we are... the Court Circular... let me see, now... I wonder if I might just take this with me... of course I know it is not my turn until Saturday, but I would return it tomorrow...

MISS MATTY. But tomorrow is Thursday... and Mr. Hoggins calls for it regularly every Thursday afternoon... and I was thinking perhaps I should just read up the Court news myself before Mr. Hoggins takes it...

MISS POLE (*moving* U.R., *struck by a thought*). Mr. Hoggins! God bless my soul... how terrible... tomorrow afternoon...!

MISS MATTY (*innocently*). Tomorrow is Thursday, is it not?

MISS POLE. And does he not always stay for a cup of tea...?

MISS MATTY. Very often...

MISS POLE. Then do you not see? Mr. Hoggins might actually be here when Lady Glenmire arrives...!

MISS MATTY. Oh dear...!

MARY. But perhaps a gentleman might add to the party...

MISS POLE. That is just the point, dear Mary... Mr. Hoggins is not a gentleman...

MARY. Is he not the doctor...?

MISS POLE. That does not signify. His family were... well, very ordinary people... in fact I am afraid we must admit they were common...

MISS MATTY. But very respectable...

MISS POLE. And what is more, Mrs. Jamieson quite refuses to meet him socially... after all, with a name like Hoggins .... it might almost as well be Piggins...

MISS MATTY. Poor Mr. Hoggins...

MISS POLE. Only think of introducing him to Her Ladyship ... "Lady Glenmire, may I present Mr. *Hoggins*"! (*Shrugs her shoulders and turns again to the St. James's Chronicle.*) Well, now!... "Her Majesty Queen Adelaide appeared wearing one of the new turbans..."

MISS MATTY (*eagerly*). Sea green... satin...

MISS POLE. "And was complimented by the King on the becoming nature of her head-dress"... fancy that... A turban!

MISS MATTY. But very unsuitable for Cranford...

MISS POLE. Oh... quite... quite unsuitable... Thank

you for the paper . . . and now I will be running along . . .
I must speak to Mrs. Forrester.

(*The doorbell is heard again.* MISS POLE *darts to the window and inspects the caller with a professional eye.*)

MISS MATTY. Who is it . . . ?

(MARTHA *crosses from* D.R. *to hall.*)

MISS POLE. Miss Betty Barker . . . all out of breath. She has heard about Lady Glenmire, I dare say . . . and is all in a state about it . . . poor thing.

MISS B. (*off*). Is Miss Matilda Jenkyns at home . . . ?

MARTHA (*off. Affirmatively*). Aye. (*But she makes no move.*)

MISS B. (*off*). I wonder if you would kindly inform her that Miss Barker, Miss Betty Barker, would much appreciate a few moments' conversation with her . . . ?

MARTHA (*appearing from passage*). There's a body wants to talk to you . . .

MISS MATTY. Oh dear . . . that girl! (*Then, raising her voice.*) Come in, dear Miss Barker . . . come in . . .

MISS B. (*entering and crossing* L. *of sofa*). I trust you will see fit to excuse this unwarrantable intrusion, Miss Jenkyns . . . but I come on a matter of excessive importance . . . in fact, I may say that I bear news!

(*Exit* MARTHA *to kitchen.*)

MISS MATTY. Miss Barker . . . here is our dear Mary come to pay me another visit . . . is it not kind of her?

MISS B. Oh, excessively kind . . . though what an honour, indeed, to stay with dear Miss Jenkyns . . . How do you do, Miss Mary . . . may I, very humbly, bid you welcome to Cranford . . . ?

MARY. How are you, Miss Barker?

(*They shake hands.*)

MISS POLE (*advancing from the window recess where she has remained unseen. She speaks sharply*). Good morning, Miss Barker . . . you seem very out of breath . . .

MISS B. (*who obviously does not care for Miss Pole*). Oh! Miss Pole . . .

MISS MATTY. Pray sit down, Miss Barker, and tell us your

news...

Miss B. (*sitting* L.C. *and taking a deep breath*). Then I must tell you, ladies, that Cranford is in the receipt of a most signal honour; an event, I may say, almost without precedence has occurred here in our midst. And on this occasion, feeling in need of leadership, I turn of course to dear Miss Jenkyns... the daughter of our late rector and the centre, I think I may say, of our little society... (*She bows to* Miss M.)

Miss Matty. Thank you, Miss Barker... but...

Miss B. And believe me, I am not unaware of the presumption which I... which I...

Miss Pole. Presume...?

Miss B. I thank you, Miss Pole. I was about to say that I am conscious of the honour I have in being the first to communicate this intelligence to Miss Jenkyns...

Miss Matty (*sitting with* Miss P. *on sofa.*) Let us waive formality, Miss Barker... and hear your news...

Miss B. Ladies! We have amongst us... in our humble, though genteel society, a visitor... a member of the peerage...!

(*She pauses for the expected gasp of surprise.*)

Miss Pole (*in an artificially casual tone, robs her at one stroke of her triumph*). Oh...? You refer to Mrs. Jamieson's sister-in-law, I suppose?

Miss B. (*horribly crestfallen*). You know...? You already know... about *Lady* Glenmire...?

Miss Pole (*disgustingly superior*). Some such name as that: ...I declare, I have almost forgot...

Miss B. (*pathetically*). Oh dear... and I hurried so... to be the first to tell you...

Miss Matty (*kindly*). That was exceedingly considerate of you, Miss Barker, and I take it very kindly...

Miss B. And she will be here...? Tomorrow? To tea?

Miss Pole. Naturally.

Miss B. I must admit that I am a little behind-hand these days in my knowledge of occurrences in high society... and I wondered if I might just glance at the latest copy of the

St. James's Chronicle ... I know it is not my turn ... but ...

MISS MATTY. Certainly ... Miss Pole has it at the moment ...

MISS POLE (*annoyed at being caught with it*). Why ... so I have ... I was just glancing at ... (*She catches* MISS MATTY's *eye.*) Oh, well ... the fact of the matter is that I cannot correctly recall the mode of addressing a Lady ... so silly of me ... just slipped my mind ...

(MISS P. *hands the* St. James's Chronicle *to* MISS B.)

MISS B. (*taking the paper*). Now that ... Miss Matty, is my own predicament. I was sure that you could help me, being, as everybody knows, a connection of Sir Peter and Lady Arley ...

MISS POLE. It is really a question of whether one says, *My Lady* instead of *Ma'am* ...

(MISS BARKER *studies the paper.*)

MARY. Or one might say "Good afternoon, Lady Glenmire".

MISS MATTY. Why, so indeed one might ... How clever of you, dear, to think of it ...

MISS POLE. Or, "Good afternoon, Your Ladyship".

MISS MATTY (*to* MARY). My dear, if they fix on that you must let me practise a little on you first.

MISS B. (*looking up from* Chronicle). Dear Queen Adelaide appeared in a turban ... Hmmm——

MISS MATTY (*longingly*). Yes ... sea-green ...

MARY. But most unsuitable for Cranford ...

MISS MATTY. Oh ... of course ... almost vulgar ...

MISS POLE. Naturally ...

MISS B. Just what I was about to say ...

MISS MATTY. I am afraid the Chronicle is no help in the matter of addressing the nobility. We were thinking, when you arrived, Miss Barker, of inquiring of Mrs. Forrester ...

MISS POLE. Whose father was a soldier ...

MISS MATTY. And fought against Napoleon ... (*She delivers this triumphantly as if that settled the matter.*)

MISS B. Of course ... And we can never forget that she was born a Tyrrell ... and is allied to the Bigges, of Bigelow Hall ...

Miss Pole. Though her circumstances are sadly changed...
Miss Matty. Poor Mrs. Forrester...
   (*The doorbell is heard again.*)
Miss Pole (*darting to the window*). I thought so... It is Mrs. Forrester...
   (*She turns to* Martha *who has appeared at the kitchen door.*)
Never mind, Martha, it is but Mrs. Forrester, and I will let her in...
   (*Exit* Martha... Miss Pole *lets in* Mrs. Forrester ... she is rather older than the other ladies... and is comfortably fat. She is not very expensively dressed... in fact... rather plainly so... She has a pleasant, kindly face...*)
Mrs. F. Oh! Miss Pole... Is Miss Matty in...?
   (Miss P. *moves and sits on chair* D.R.)
Miss Matty. Dear Mrs. Forrester... come in...
Mrs. F. (*moving to* C. *and looking round at them all*). There now ... I can see by your faces that you already know... Why—here's Miss Mary—
Mary. How are you, Mrs. Forrester...?
   (Mrs. F. *sits* L. *of* Miss M.)
Miss Matty. You are in time to help us, Mrs. Forrester... we are most perplexed as to the correct mode of addressing a member of the peerage...
Mrs. F. Why, indeed... that is exactly what I was going to ask you...
Miss B. (*who is even more of a snob than the others*). Yes, Mrs. Forrester...
Miss Pole (*almost accusingly*). And, if I remember rightly, your father was an officer under Wellington...
Miss Matty. And defeated Napoleon... at Waterloo...
Miss B. And I have frequently heard you tell how he was personally congratulated, after the battle, by the Duchess of Wellington herself...
Mrs. F. (*wincing under this attack*). That may be... but he did not inform me how to address a countess...
Miss Pole (*sniffing*). Humph...!
Mrs. F. (*quite sharply for one so soft*). And if my memory

does not deceive me, Miss Pole, your uncle, on your mother's side, was a colonel in the Army and fought under General Burgoyne in the American war ...

MISS MATTY (*sincerely ... for she is always kind*). Why, so he was, Miss Pole ...

MISS POLE. That was quite different.

MRS. F. Oh yes, of course ... we won the war in France ... and we lost the war in America ...

(MISS POLE *is about to reply with warmth when* MARY *speaks.*)

MARY (*anxious to change the subject*). Miss Matty ... I think I remember seeing a copy of the "Peerage" on your bookshelf ... perhaps it might help us ...

MISS MATTY. My dear, how clever you are ... of course, the very thing ... it's in the dining-room ... a large book with a brown paper cover ...

(MARY *is about to fetch it when the doorbell rings again.* MISS POLE *as usual, is first to the window.*)

MISS POLE (*in violent excitement*). It is Mrs. Jamieson's coachman ...; her carriage is at the gate ...

(*There is a chorus of twittering from the ladies who all rise to their feet and run about like chickens.*)

MISS MATTY (*rising*). Oh dear ... oh dear ... they are coming to call ...

(MARY *picks up the newspapers off the carpet.*)

MISS POLE. Mrs. Jamieson is getting out of her carriage ...

MISS B. (*to fireplace*). And Her Ladyship ... ? Is she there too?

MRS. F. (*to* D.R.). Miss Matty ... would you object very much if I left by the back door ... ? I am afraid I am not dressed for company ...

MISS POLE. She is coming up the path ...

MISS MATTY. Mrs. Forrester ... Ladies! I pray you ... do not desert me ...

MISS POLE (*returning to the room*). Perhaps if I might just pop into your dining-room ... and study your copy of the "Peerage".

(*The bell rings again.*)

MISS B. I have just remembered that I have a most urgent

errand... most urgent... the back door...
MARY. I wonder where Martha can be...
MISS MATTY. Martha... oh goodness me... where can she be?
   (*Enter* MARTHA *carrying a bucket and mop... she proceeds to door.*)
Martha...! Martha...! Wait for the cough...
   (MARTHA *halts uncertainly and shoulders her broom.*)
MISS POLE (*moving* R. *and taking command*). Ladies! I am sure we would not for the world leave Miss Matty alone at a time like this...
   (*They rally round her like soldiers round a leader... there is a chorus of "Not-for-the-world".*)
MISS MATTY. I thank you, ladies.
MISS POLE. Nor would we embarrass Miss Matty by the lack of... er... elegance in our morning costumes...
MISS B. Beautifully expressed...
MISS POLE. I therefore suggest that we should wait for a short while in the dining-room where Miss Matty will have the benefit of our moral support... and will be at the same time saved from embarrassment...
MRS. F. Splendid idea...
   (*With which they abandon formality and scuttle for the door in almost indecent haste.* MISS P., MISS B., *and* MRS. F. *exeunt* D.R.)
MISS MATTY (*moving* L.) Oh dear... they've gone... they've left me...
MARY. There, Miss Matty... it is nothing very serious...
   (*She leads her to a chair... and hands her the book.*)
MISS MATTY. Thank you, my dear. I must try to remember that I am the Rector's daughter... that might help... (*She is almost composed when she sees* MARTHA *and the bucket.*) My goodness... look... she's got a bucket...!
MARY. Leave that to me.
   (*She crosses behind* MISS M. *to* MARTHA, *who is, or appears to be, paralysed, straightens her cap... takes the bucket, and the mop from her, and retreats to the kitchen door, where she pauses... dives back into the room and collects the papers... then—*)

Now...!
> (*Exit* MARY *with bucket and mop. So* MISS MATTY *is left alone at this great moment... however, she coughs with considerable, though tremulous, dignity. Then, like an automaton,* MARTHA *opens the door and we hear the voice of the* COACHMAN... *Off...*)

MARTHA (*repeating like a parrot*). The Honourable Mrs. Jamieson...
> (*And in sweeps* MRS. JAMIESON *to* C. *below sofa. She is an elderly woman... much inflated by fat and by her own sense of importance... She is opulently dressed.*)

MISS MATTY (*laying down her book and rising*). Why... Mrs. Jamieson... How kind of you to call... (*She peers towards the hall.*) Are you... are you alone?

MRS. J. Good morning, Miss Jenkyns... Certainly I am alone...

MISS MATTY (*heaving a sigh of relief*). That will be all, Martha.
> (MARTHA *closes the door and marches across the room like a robot and goes out to kitchen.*)

MISS MATTY. Pray take a seat, Mrs. Jamieson. (MRS. J. *sits on sofa.*) A lovely day... How lucky we are to enjoy such weather so late in the season...

MRS. J. (*seating herself*). I called upon you, Miss Jenkyns, with reference to a visitor I have in my home...

MISS MATTY. Is that so...?

MRS. J. It is so. The visitor happens to be my sister-in-law... the widow of my late husband's brother... also defunct. You may perhaps be acquainted with the fact that my late husband's brother was the late Earl of Glenmire...? (MISS MATTY *inclines her head.*) It follows then that my sister-in-law is the Dowager Countess of Glenmire...

MISS MATTY. Excessively interèsting...

MRS. J. Lady Glenmire will be making a stay of some little time in Cranford...

MISS MATTY. I'm sure we shall all make her welcome, m'am...

MRS. J. Ah...! That is what I wish to speak to you about. You understand, of course, that my sister-in-law is accustomed to mix with the highest society?

MISS MATTY. I am sure of that, m'am ...
MRS. J.. And, of course, while I have been a resident of Cranford, I have seen no harm in mixing to some extent with the small society of the place ... in fact, I think I may claim to have behaved on all occasions in a truly democratic spirit ... (*She is beginning to get slightly uncomfortable.*)
MISS MATTY (*uncompromising*). Indeed, ma'am ...
MRS. J. In short ... you must understand I could not expect Lady Glenmire to make the same condescension ...
MISS MATTY (*rising and moving* U. C.). That will be very simple, Madam ... if Lady Glenmire wishes to live a life of seclusion at Cranford I think I may promise you that nobody will break in upon her privacy ...
MRS. J. Of course I do not mean to say that ...
MISS MATTY. Of course not. As I was saying, what lovely weather we are having for the season ... though a trifle cold for your coachman to wait so long ...
   (MISS MATTY *crosses to window.*)
MRS. J. (*rises and moves to fireplace*). Yes ... yes ... I must be going ... my coachman is subject to the rheumatics. You understand, of course ... about your little tea-party tomorrow ... that owing to ... I shall be forced to decline.
   (MRS. J. *crosses towards the front door.*)
MISS MATTY (*leading the way to the front door*). And be sure and tell the poor man to place red flannel on the afflicted spot ... it is a sure preventive, I do assure you, ma'am ...
   (MISS MATTY "*bobs*".)
MRS. J. Thank you. Good day to you, Miss Jenkyns ...
   (*Exit* MRS. JAMIESON.)
MISS MATTY (*off*). Good day to you ... Mrs. Jamieson ...
   (*She closes the door and returns to the parlour. At once the ladies,* MISS POLE, MISS BARBER *and* MRS. FORRESTER *come in a flood from* D.R.)
MISS POLE. Well ... ! I never heard the like of it!
   (*There is a chorus of cries of shocked horror and outrage.*)
MISS MATTY. And now we shall never know if she wears a turban!

     CURTAIN.

ACT ONE
Scene II

SET. *The same.*

TIME. *Late afternoon of the following day.*

AT RISE. *We see that preparations are well in hand for the tea party. A satin-wood card table has been set up for four players ... Small vases of flowers give a slightly festive air and candle-sticks one on mantelpiece and one on small table D. L., each with two out of five candles lit. A small fire burns in the grate. At this moment* MARY *is checking over the arrangements and placing packs of cards and scoring pads on the card table. Enter* MARTHA *from the dining-room carrying two dining chairs to complete the set at the table ... two being already in place.)*

MARY. Thank you, Martha ... that's right ... just there.
  (*She places the chairs formally round the table.*)
  And remember, when Miss Matty rings the bell ... bring in first the tea-tray ... and place it on that table there. (*She indicates a side-table.*) Then I will start to pour the tea, and you will bring in the bread and butter and sponge fingers ...

MARTHA. And what about the gentlemen? You aren't a'going to give them tea ...?

MARY. There will be no gentlemen present, Martha.

MARTHA. That's a shame ... myself, I like the lads best.

MARY. While we are on this subject, Martha, I think Miss Matty would like me to speak to you on the subject of followers ...

MARTHA (*intensely interested*). Ah, now!

MARY. Because you must understand, Martha, that while you work in this house they must be absolutely forbidden ... It need not ever be discussed again provided you understand completely ... No followers ...

MARTHA. Followers? But please, Miss ... I never had more nor one at a time.

MARY. Martha!

ACT I, SCENE 2] CRANFORD 33

MARTHA (*to below sofa*). Very well, Miss. Though it do seem hard on a girl. If you ask me, Miss Jenkyns herself would have done better to take Mr. Holbrook when he offered for her...

MARY (*to whom this is news*). Mr. Holbrook? What are you talking about... who is he?

MARTHA. He lives a ways out... in the country. My mother used to do for him, days. She said as how everybody knew he was sweet on Miss Matty years ago and many's the time she's seen him looking at a lock of her hair in the back of his watch...

MARY. The first thing you must learn, Martha... is never to gossip about your employer.

(*The doorbell rings.*)

MARY. Oh dear... Here they come and it is not yet half past five. Quickly, Martha... the candles...

(MARTHA *runs round lighting candles while* MARY *draws the curtains. Presently* MARTHA *goes to the window for the usual inspection...*)

You need not bother with the window this evening, Martha, we know who our guests will be... I wonder if Miss Matty is finished cutting the bread and butter.

(*The voice of* MISS POLE *is heard through the letter-box.*)

MISS POLE (*off*). It is only I... Miss Pole...

(MARY *nods to* MARTHA *who opens the door... and in bounces* MISS POLE... *she is wearing a cape and, over her head, a calash, which is a large covering designed to be worn over caps... she also carries a large book.*)

Good evening, Mary... I know I am too early but do not disturb yourselves for me. I have just found out all about Lady Glenmire in this copy of the "Peerage" and could not wait to read it to you...

MARY. Take Miss Pole's calash, Martha... and put it in the hall room.

(MISS POLE *removes her outer coverings and hands them to* MARTHA *who takes them to hall,* MISS P. *chattering the while.*)

MISS POLE. Of course, it is no more than I expected... and

I said as much to Betty yesterday..."Member of the Peerage", I said, "Well, there's peerage...and then again there's peerage..."
(During this time MISS MATTY *peeps out of the kitchen door...wiping her hands on a cloth. She pops the cloth back into the kitchen and a second later descends the front stairs as if just coming from her bedroom.)*
MISS MATTY. Good evening, Miss Pole...how kind of you to come early...
(Exit MARTHA.*)*
MISS POLE *(moving* U. C. *as they come down stage).* I felt I had to let you know how we have been imposed upon by this *(Moves below sofa.)* Lady Glenmire, who is to be kept under a glass case...I have it all here in the book...
MISS MATTY (R. *below sofa).* I really feel it might be more dignified not to discuss the lady at all.
MISS POLE *(sitting on sofa).* And that is exactly what I feel too...which is the reason why I came early so that I might tell you before the others get here. *(She seats herself and opens the book.)* Now, Lady Glenmire, I will have you know... is nothing more than the widow of a Scottish peer...!
MISS MATTY. But a real earl, nonetheless...
MISS POLE *(sniffing).* But never sat in the House of Lords... and as poor as Job I dare say...and my Lady Glenmire no more than the fifth daughter of some Mr. Campbell or other...who nobody ever heard of...
MISS MATTY. Well, Lady Glenmire...whoever her father may have been...has not personally injured me...and she may be a very good sort of woman for all I know...
MISS POLE. I for one will show Mrs. Jamieson...that I don't give a fig for her fine relations... *(The doorbell is heard. Enter* MARTHA U.C.... *she looks enquiringly at* MISS MATTY.) ...and if she was to come to me on bended knees and beseech me to meet My Lady...I'd...well...I'd show her that you cannot trifle with a Pole...!
MISS MATTY. Open the door, Martha...it will be Miss Barker and Mrs. Forrester.
*(*MARTHA *goes to the front door and we hear a man's voice*

off... it is MR. HOGGINS.)
MR. H. (*off*). Is Miss Matilda Jenkyns at home?
MARTHA. I'll see... but we haven't laid for a gentleman...
MISS POLE (*rising and crossing to* R.). It's Mr. Hoggins!
MISS MATTY (*moving* U. C. *below sofa*). Come for the St. James's Chronicle...
MISS POLE. I suppose it does not matter since we have no high society...
MISS MATTY (*she raises her voice*). Come in, Mr. Hoggins.
MISS POLE (*sotto voce*). Hoggins! What a name, to be sure.
 (*Enter* MR. HOGGINS... *he is a tall, jovial-looking man. A little rough-and-ready in his manners, but a pleasant individual.*)
  (MARTHA *stays off by front door.*)
MR. H. Good evening to you, ma'am... I have come for the Chronicle... My day for it, Thursday, you will remember...
MISS MATTY. Oh yes, Mr. Hoggins... I had thought to send Martha over with it but it slipped my memory.
MR. H. Don't apologise, ma'am... don't apologise... A pleasure to visit you and these lovely ladies...
MISS MATTY. This is Miss Mary Smith... I do not recollect if you have met before...?
  (HOGGINS *crosses to* MARY.)
MARY. How do you do, Mr. Hoggins?
  (*They shake hands.*)
MR. H. A pleasure... a pleasure, indeed. (*Crossing* D. R.) And the fair Miss Pole?
  (MISS POLE *sniffs but does not speak.*)
MISS MATTY. I was just expecting a few ladies for tea and a game of preference...
MR. H. (*moving up to* MISS P.). What...? More beauty...? Upon my word... your parlour is a dangerous place for a lonely bachelor...
MISS POLE. You have never been more secure in your life, sir.
MR. H. (*not in the least put out*). Ha... ha!
MISS POLE (*crosses... picks up the Chronicle and hands it to him*).

Here, sir, is the Chronicle. I shall be glad if you will keep it out of your surgery, for last week when it came to me it distinctly smelled of ether...

MR. H. I am sorry, ma'am... but a surgeon is a busy man ... he cannot be always in his parlour...

MISS POLE. You mean you study Court news while extracting the teeth of your victims?

MR. H. (*laughing*). Ah, ha... Miss Pole... I see you are as much of a tease as ever... But no... I have never so much as looked at the Court news... it is those capital Pickwick Papers I read...

MISS POLE (*with fearful disgust*). Pickwick Papers...!

MR. H. I declare I can hardly wait for the next number. Have you read this week's issue, Miss Jenkyns? (MISS M. *moves towards him.*) Can you tell me what tricks Sam Weller is up to in Bath...?

MISS MATTY. I am afraid I must tell you, sir, that low, modern literature is never read in this house. My sister and my father both considered that Doctor Johnson was the most improving writer imaginable... and he is still good enough for me...

MISS POLE. Pickwick Papers, indeed... by Mr. Boz... the very name is enough...

MR. H. I hear his name is really Dickens... and his writing, ma'am... I consider famously good and should not be compared with Dr. Johnson... it is quite a different thing.

(*Enter* MARTHA *from front door... she carries a small note on a silver salver.*)

MARTHA. Here's a letter, ma'am... for you... A gentleman brought it.

MISS MATTY. How strange. Excuse me, please...

(MR. HOGGINS *retires to the baywindow* (R.) *and the ladies become politely unaware that a letter is being read.* MISS MATTY *tears it open and reads the contents... she gives a gasp and sits down very suddenly.*)

MARY (*to sofa*). Miss Matty! Is something wrong...?

MISS MATTY. Yes. (*She silently hands the note to* MARY.)

MISS POLE (*to* MISS MATTY, *anxiously*). Nothing serious, I hope?
MISS MATTY (*to* MARY). Read it, my dear . . . read it aloud . . .
MARY (*reading*). "The Honourable Mrs. Jamieson presents her compliments . . . she has given a certain matter further thought . . . and will wait upon Miss Jenkyns this afternoon for tea and cards . . . together with her sister-in-law, Lady Glenmire." (*She sits on sofa.*)
MR. H. (*he has moved* U. L.—*has been deep in Pickwick, gives a laugh . . . the ladies start in surprise . . . but he continues*). That's a good one . . . Sam Weller, off to a 'swarry' . . . upon my soul . . . !
   (*But he goes on reading to himself . . . the ladies shrug their shoulders and talk among themselves.*)
MISS MATTY. Of course, I shall reply that we have made up our table for preference, and that it will be inconvenient.
MARY. Yes. I'll get you some paper and a pen . . .
MISS POLE. Wait a minute, ladies . . . perhaps it would be better to give this matter a little thought . . .
MISS MATTY. But you, yourself, Miss Pole, this very minute said that if Mrs. Jamieson was to come on her bended knees . . .
MISS POLE. Perhaps I spoke in anger . . . Remember the great Christian principle, forgive and forget . . .
MISS MATTY. I think I should prefer to forget Mrs. Jamieson first . . . and then forgive her!
MISS POLE. And again . . . it would be too flattering to her to allow her to suppose that what she had said on one day . . . we even remembered on the next!
MARY. Perhaps it would be better, Miss Matty . . . to overlook Mrs. Jamieson's behaviour . . . after all, you have known her for a long time and are used to her ways . . .
MISS POLE. Of course, and you know she cannot help the fact that she does not entertain the little delicacies of feeling that you possess in so remarkable a degree . . .
MISS MATTY. But I thought that you possessed these delicacies of feeling, Miss Pole?
MISS POLE. Ah, yes . . . I know I am far too sensitive . . . and that is why I have always taken you, Miss Jenkyns, as

my model of Christian forbearance...
MISS MATTY (*making up her mind*). Very well... it shall be as you say... I wonder if she'll wear a turban...!
MISS POLE (*rising quickly and looking in a mirror*). Oh, my goodness... yes... I wonder...
  (MARTHA *moves* D.C.)
MISS MATTY (*to* MARTHA). You may tell Mrs. Jamieson's butler that I shall be happy to receive his mistress and her visitor...
MARTHA. Tell him? But he's gone... said there was no need to wait for an answer... the ladies'll be along in a minute.
  (*Exit* MARTHA D.R. MISS POLE *gives a slight scream.*)
MISS MATTY. Oh dear, and we never decided what to call her..
MISS POLE (*after another look in mirror*). There now...! And if I didn't forget to tell my Betty to... to feed the cat...!
MISS MATTY. The cat...?
MISS POLE. Poor pussy will be famished... You must excuse me if I just run back home for a minute... (*She suddenly remembers Hoggins.*) And what are you going to do about...? (*She points to him... he is still deeply immersed in Pickwick.*)
MISS MATTY (*distressed*). Oh dear... what can I do?
MARY (*moving* D. R.). I must remind Martha to put two more cups on the tea tray...
MR. H. (*looking up suddenly*). Tea? Did I hear the word tea...?
MISS POLE. You did, sir... and I have no doubt you must be hurrying home for yours.
MISS MATTY (*shocked at such rudeness*). Oh no, Miss Pole...
MR. H. Then, since you press me, ma'am... I shall be delighted to stay...
MARY. *Three* more cups...
  (*Exit* MARY *to kitchen.*)
MISS POLE (*in a hoarse aside*). Now... you've done it... ma'am...
MISS MATTY. A matter of delicacy of feeling, ma'am...!
MISS POLE. Well, I must not forget poor pussy... kindness to dumb animals, you know... I shall be back in one minute...

(*She is making for the front door and her calash when the doorbell rings... Both ladies are turned to stone... after a pause* MISS P. *recovers herself.*)
I'll slip out the back way and across the garden... quicker that way...

MISS MATTY (*almost pleading*). Miss Pole... I beg of you...

MISS POLE (*literally racing for the kitchen door*). Poor, dear pussy...

(*Exit* MISS POLE... *Enter* MARTHA.)

MISS MATTY (*seating herself in a semblance of composure...*). Very well, Martha... (*She pronounces this in the manner of a victim of the guillotine giving the last word to the executioner...* MARTHA *proceeds up the hall to the door.*) Mr.... Mr. Hoggins...! A lovely day...!

(*Trying tremulously to be absorbed in conversation...* MR. HOGGINS *looks up...*)

MR. H. Your pardon, ma'am?

(MARTHA *opens the door and in step* MISS BARKER *and* MRS. FORRESTER... MARTHA *helps them to remove their calashes... as they do not speak and as* MISS MATTY *is far too nervous to peep... she continues her inane conversation...*)

MISS MATTY. Such lovely sunshine...

MR. H. (*glancing at the drawn curtains*). It is dark, madam...

MISS MATTY (*flatly*). Oh yes... dark. (*Then with a new idea.*) But in other parts of the world, they tell me the sun shines when it is dark here...

(*Enter* MISS BARKER *and* MRS. FORRESTER... *escorted by* MARTHA *having removed their wraps.*)

MARTHA. The ladies, ma'am...

MISS MATTY (*jumping as if shot and moving to* R. *of sofa*). Oh..! (*She sees who it is.*) Oh... Mrs. Forrester... dear Mrs. Forrester... and Miss Barker.

(*Exit* MARTHA... MISS B. *moves to* L. *of sofa.*)

MRS. F. (*moving behind sofa*). Good afternoon, Miss Matty... How very pleasant... and a quiet game of preference.

MISS B. How I have been looking forward to this afternoon... Just a small circle of old friends...

Miss Matty. Yes, yes ... You know, Mr. Hoggins, do you not ... ?

Mr. H. (*bowing*). Good afternoon to you, ladies. Nothing more warming to the heart than a small gathering of old friends ...

Mrs. F. How right you are, sir ... (*Settling herself comfortably on* R. *end of sofa.*) For my part it is quite a relief that ... "you know who" is not coming ... Our little society in Cranford does very well without strangers ... no need to dress smartly—we can wear the same old clothes—

Miss B. (*sitting* L. *end of sofa*). And if I see her in the street I shall cut her ...

Mrs. F. Of course ... so shall I to be sure ...

Miss Matty (*moving to* C. *and nervously clearing her throat*). Ladies! I ... er ... I have some news ... I trust it will not be unpleasant ...

Mrs. F. Indeed ... ?

Miss Matty. Yes. This moment I received a note from Mrs. Jamieson to say that she and her sister-in-law would be coming here to tea ... after all ...

(*Both ladies leap directly to their feet ...*)

Miss B. (*in a high-pitched squeal*). Today!

Mrs. F. Lady Glenmire ... ?

Miss Matty. I hope you will forgive me ... but I felt it might be un-Christian to hold a grudge ...

(*Both* Miss B. *and* Mrs. F. *are not listening* ... *they are almost fighting for the mirror* ....)

Miss B. I wonder what she'll wear ...

Mrs. F. Perhaps a turban ...

Mrs. B. (*moving towards front door*). There now. If I didn't forget before I came out to tell my Peggy to lock the back door ... If you will excuse me, Miss Matty ... I will just run home and ...

Mrs. F. (*moving towards front door*). How odd ... now you mention it ... I clean forgot to tell my Jenny to fasten the windows ...

Miss B. Several cases of burglary of late . . .
>(*By this time they are crowding for the door . . . deaf to* Miss Matty's *little cries of distress . . .*)

Miss Matty. Ladies . . . please . . . ! I pray you . . . !
>(*The doorbell rings again, the ladies are again rooted to the spot.*)

Miss B. (*breathlessly*). It's them . . . I mean, they . . .

Mrs. F. Too late . . . !
>(*Enter* Martha, *followed by* Mary. *The ladies come down centre . . .* Mary *joins* Miss Matty *and takes her hand . . .* Martha *proceeds to the door . . .*)

Miss Matty. Wait a minute, Martha . . .
>(Martha *pauses at the door.*)

Pray seat yourselves, ladies . . .
>(*Everybody, with the exception of* Mr. Hoggins, *sits down . . . and there they perch like so many ramrods.*)

Martha . . . !
>(Miss Matty *sits at top of card table.*)

You may open the door.
>(Martha *disappears and we hear the door opening and the sound of voices. Also the words* (*off*) "Mrs. Jamieson and Lady Glenmire". *There is a deathly silence on stage until* Miss Matty *rallies and starts another forced conversation.*)

Mr. Hoggins, I believe you were making an interesting observation on the subject of our colonies . . . ?

Mr. H. Was I now, madam . . . ?

Miss Matty. Ah . . . the colonies . . . a great source of satisfaction to the dear King . . .

Mrs. F. And to the dear Queen . . . I am sure . . .

Miss B. And may I inquire, Miss Jenkyns, what is your latest news from Court?

Miss Matty. Oh dear . . . I think the colonies are safer . . .

Mr. H. Interesting things, colonies . . .
>(*There is another deep silence while they all strain their ears desperately toward the curtain. Presently we hear them advancing along the hall . . . and there is another desperate effort at casual chat.*)

(MARTHA *draws aside the curtain.*)
MARTHA. Here they are, ma'am . . .
  (MISS MATTY *rises with dignity and advances to meet them. Enter* MRS. JAMIESON *and* LADY GLENMIRE. MRS. J. *is much the same as before, except that she wears, like the others, a lace cap.* LADY GLENMIRE . . . *is a quick-moving personage . . . very plainly dressed in black silk . . . and also wearing a a lace cap. She is bright, cheerful and smiling—very attractive for her age, which is also "over thirty-five".*)
MISS MATTY (*with a dignity that never deserts her at times of need*). How do you do, ma'am . . . and is this your sister-in-law . . .?
MRS. J. May I present Miss Jenkyns . . . Lady Glenmire . . .
MISS MATTY. A pleasure, ma'am . . . And let me introduce my friends?
LADY G. (*a very faint Scotch accent*). Indeed it's a pleasure for me, Miss Jenkyns . . . to meet yourself and all the ladies of Cranford . . . I would give Mrs. Jamieson, here, no rest till I could meet you . . .
MISS MATTY. You are very kind, madam. Now here is Mrs. Forrester . . . Lady Glenmire . . .
MRS. F. (*bobs up and down like a jack-in-the-box*). Your servant, ma'am . . .
MISS MATTY. And Miss Betty Barker . . . Lady Glenmire . . .
MISS B. (*rising and giving a half-curtsey*). An honour, your ladyship . . . (*Having been the first to get it out . . . she glances in triumph at* MRS. F.)
MISS MATTY. And my young friend, Miss Mary Smith . . . though we all call her just "Mary" . . . Lady Glenmire . . .
LADY G. How are you, my dear . . . How nice and young and bonny you look . . .
MISS MATTY (*approaching* MR. HOGGINS). And this is . . . this is Mr. . . . (*She looks wildly for help.*)
MR. H. Hoggins, madam . . . Hoggins with an aitch and two gees . . . at your service, ma'am . . .
LADY G. (*crossing to* HOGGINS). How do you do, Mr. Hoggins? I used to know some Hoggins back in Edinburgh a while ago . . .
MR. H. Did you, now?

MRS. J. (*occupying* MISS M.'*s previous chair. She has nodded to the ladies and seated herself comfortably, strong disapproval in her voice*). Is Mr. Hoggins here for tea?
MISS MATTY. He is, Mrs. Jamieson . . .
MRS. J. (*turning her chair away*). How strange.
LADY G. (*sitting* D. L., *taking chair offered by* MR. H.). Now is this not a cosy circle . . .
   (*Everybody is now seated and again there is an uncomfortable pause.*)
MISS B. (*making a superhuman effort*). I expect you will find Cranford very quiet, ma'am, after the society of London . . .
LADY G. London? Why, I was only in London but twice in my life . . . and that was many a year ago . . .
MRS. J. The late Earl was fond of a retired life . . .
LADY G. Why, as to that . . . we could never afford London . . . It was as much as we could do to visit Edinburgh now and again . . .
   (*There is a pause of amazement while this sinks in . . . and* MRS. J. *gets several nasty looks.*)
Ye'll have been in Edinburgh, maybe?
MRS. F. Indeed . . . what a coincidence . . . I once had an uncle on my mother's side who visited Edinburgh . . . He declared it was a very pleasant city . . .
   (*Another pause . . . for this topic is obviously dead.*)
LADY G. But I think Cranford very pleasant . . . and cheaper too, they tell me . . . Do you know that just before I left Scotland the price of sugar had risen beyond all belief?
   (*They all feel happier now.*)
MISS MATTY. Now is that so?
LADY G. It was all but impossible to put up my preserves in the autumn . . .
MISS MATTY. I have a recipe for preserves that calls for remarkably little sugar, ma'am . . . I always use it myself . . .
LADY G. Then before I leave Cranford I shall beg you to give it me, ma'am . . . Is it for plums . . . ?
MISS B. It is indeed . . .
LADY G. Now I wonder if anybody here has a recipe for kedgeree . . . ?

MISS MATTY. How strange, ma'am, that you should mention kedgeree, for I have the most excellent recipe that was sent by a cousin all the way from India...
MRS. J. I do not care for kedgeree.
LADY G. Then you have not had it properly made. I shall make you some this very week... Can one obtain good salted codfish here in Cranford...?
MISS B. Oh, the very best, ma'am... I will speak to the fishmonger myself and have him lay aside a good piece for you...
LADY G. That is most kind... I shall remember...
MISS MATTY. Of course, the cod must lie in water overnight...
   (*The doorbell rings.* MARTHA *enters from kitchen and we see her go across to the hall.*)
MRS. F. I always say that the delicacy of the kedgeree lies in the quality of the rice...
MISS B. Ah... but it all depends on the cod.
   (*We hear the door open and a few rather sharp words from* MISS POLE *off.*)
MISS POLE (*off*). Announce me, girl... don't just stand there...
   (*With which the curtains are drawn back and* MARTHA *steps into the room... still showing no sign of* MISS POLE.)
MARTHA (*startled*). Miss Pole... (*She flees to the kitchen.*)
   (*At this... like a galleon in full sail,* MISS POLE *sweeps grandly into the room. She describes a graceful curve and comes to a halt before the circle of ladies where she sinks in an elaborate curtsey. She is wearing the same dress, but it is bedecked with many small bows of ribbon and bits of lace... No less than seven brooches adorn her person... and... on her head is a sea-green satin turban.*)
MR. H. Bless my soul... if it isn't Miss Pole... and she's changed her top-knot!
   (MISS POLE *darts a lethal glance at him.*)
MISS MATTY. Sea-green... too...!
MISS POLE (*moving to* C., *playing the society lady*). La, ma'am! I am afraid I am a little late... but such a quantity of things

as I had to do... I declare, I began to wonder if I could come at all.

MISS MATTY. Lady Glenmire... This is my friend and neighbour, Miss Pole... Miss Pole, Lady Glenmire...

MISS POLE (*with another curtsey*). Your servant, ma'am...

LADY G. Verra pleased to meet ye... Miss Pole...

MISS POLE (*sitting L. C., taking in the rest of the room*). Good afternoon, ladies. (*She seats herself next to* LADY G.) Your ladyship... I'm prodigious glad to meet you... I am all impatience to hear the latest news from Court... tell me, how was Her Majesty looking when you saw her last?

LADY G. Sure, and I wouldn't be knowing, Miss Pole, for I have never seen the lady in my life...

MISS MATTY (*kind as ever*). Lady Glenmire has been telling us she has been seldom to London... but has lived a quiet life in Scotland...

LADY G. I'm afraid ye'll find me but dull company, Miss Pole. But the ladies here have been taking pity on me and giving advice upon the quality of salted cod...

MISS POLE (*coming down with a bump*). Cod!

LADY G. But such a vastly smart lady as yourself will not be knowing about such things...

MISS MATTY (*with absolute sincerity*). Oh, indeed, ma'am... you are wrong. Miss Pole is a very fine cook and you must not leave Cranford without sampling her recipe for a pickled pig's head...

MISS POLE. I... ah... I...

LADY G. Is that so? And is it in brine, ye do it, Miss Pole .... or in vinegar...?

MISS POLE (*coming back to life*). It is a very old recipe ma'am... has been in our family for a great while...

LADY G. Then I shall ask ye to cook it for me, ma'am... and have me in for supper...

MISS POLE. A pleasure, ma'am... I shall count upon it. I am sure you will not find a better recipe in Cranford... and cannot be compared with codfish. (*She gives a superior glance at* MISS B. *and* MRS. F.)

Miss B. (*viciously*). Miss Pole has many a thing you will not find the like of in Cranford ... Allow me to compliment you, Miss Pole, upon "the becoming nature of your head-dress" ...
   (*The last words she quotes with sinister meaning.*)
Lady G. Now that ye have mentioned it, ma'am ... I should like to compliment Miss Pole too ... for a smarter object I never saw ...
Miss Pole. Indeed it is nothing, ma'am ... just something I popped on in a hurry ...
Mrs. F. Miss Pole is over modest, ma'am ... it is the latest thing ... and in London they call it a turban ...
Miss Pole (*annoyed*). Thank you kindly for your information, ma'am ...
Lady G. Never you mind what they call it in London, Miss Pole ... I like it fine ... and I call it a bonnet ...
Miss Matty (*coming to the rescue*). I think, Mary dear ... you had better ring for tea ...
Mary (*rising*). Of course, Miss Matty ...
   (*She crosses and pulls the bell rope.*)
Mr. H. I have just been reading, ma'am ... the latest number of Pickwick Papers ...
Lady G. (*excitedly*). Pickwick Papers ... ? By Mr. Boz ... ? And you have the latest number ... ? Tell me quick ... what has Mr. Winkle been up to in Bath ... ?
   (*There is a shocked silence.*)
Mr. H. (*delightedly*). You are an admirer of Mr. Pickwick ... then you are a woman after my own heart ...
Lady G. Indeed, I never read anything else. And as for Mr. Pickwick ... why, I am quite in love with the old dear ...
   (*During this conversation* Martha *enters with plates of bread and butter, which she places on the appointed table. But she has not brought the tea and makes no move to fetch it ... she stands in an agony of nervousness.*)
Miss Matty. My late sister, ma'am ... and my late father too ... were great admirers of Doctor Johnson ...
Lady G. I was always told, Miss Jenkyns, that Doctor

Johnson was a very clever man ... but for myself ... I canna understand a word of it ...

MISS MATTY (*turning to* MRS. JAMIESON *who sits permanently in a majestic coma* ...). And what do you think, Mrs. Jamieson, of these Pickwick Papers ... ?

(MRS. J. *comes to life and turns upon the company a glazed stare.*)

MR. H. Yes, Mrs. Jamieson ... tell us your opinion now ... do you not agree that Mr. Snodgrass is a very funny fellow ... ?

MRS. J. (*with infinite disgust*). Snod-grass ... ?

MR. H. One of Mr. Pickwick's friends, ma'am ...

MRS. J. I have no acquaintance with the name of Pickwick ... nor of Snodgrass ...

(*There is a silence.*)

I think I will take a cup of tea ... one lump please ... and lemon ...

MISS MATTY. Oh yes ... Martha ... tea!

(MARTHA, *in deep distress, approaches* MISS MATTY *and whispers in her ear* ... MISS MATTY *gives a start and whispers to* MARY ... MARY *nods reassuringly and rises.*)

MARY (*moving to* LADY GLENMIRE). Lady Glenmire, I am sure you would like to see Miss Jenkyns' new stereoscope ... there is a view of Vesuvius in eruption which is very lifelike ...

MISS MATTY. Oh yes ... you can almost smell the smoke.

(MARY *takes up the stereoscope which is a binocular instrument with a rack for holding two identical cards, which, when the glass is clapped to the observer's eyes, appear as one* ... *and in relief* ... *she leads* LADY G. *to the window.* MISS P. *follows them.*)

LADY G. There is nothing I'd be liking more ... and a volcano too ... and in eruption ...

(*Meanwhile* MISS MATTY *whispers to* MISS B. *and* MRS. F. *who sit side by side on the sofa. In response to this they lift their knees high in the air, but continue to sit with casual dignity.* MARTHA *drops to her knees and brings forth the silver tea-tray* ... *which of course always lives under the sofa* ...

MARTHA *hurries out to the kitchen with tray.*)

LADY G. (*after a long look*). It's uncanny ... so like life ... I feel frightened.

MISS MATTY (*rising*). And now, ladies ... if we take our places at the card tables ... Martha will bring our tea.

(MRS. JAMIESON, MISS BARKER *and* MRS. FORRESTER *rise quickly and sit at the main table thus occupying three of the four places.*)

And Lady Glenmire ...? I am sure you play preference?

LADY G. (*moving to sofa and sitting on* R. *end*). I'm a pairfect fule at cards, Miss Jenkyns ... you shall take that place and I shall watch.

MISS MATTY (*dubiously*). But ...

LADY G. (*seating herself in another chair*). I insist ...

MISS MATTY. Miss Pole ...?

MISS POLE. Indeed I do not feel like cards today ... I shall chat with Lady Glenmire. (*She seizes a chair nearby.*)

(*Enter* MARTHA *with tea.*)

MARY. Do sit down, Miss Matty.... and I will help Martha serve the tea ...

MISS MATTY (*rather reluctantly taking the vacant place*). Thank you, Mary dear ... and Mr. Hoggins ... I know he will not play at cards, but ...

MR. H. (*taking the Chronicle and going to a chair in the window*). Mr. Hoggins will be very happy with Mr. Pickwick ...

(MARY *starts pouring out the tea and* MISS B. *starts to deal the cards* ... MR. HOGGINS *springs up again.*)

Allow me, Miss Mary ... I will pass the bread and butter ...

(MARY *and* MARTHA *pass around cups of tea* ... *and* MR. H. *follows with the bread and butter. Each lady absently takes a slice while sorting her cards.*)

LADY G. It is kind of ye to keep me company, ma'am ... And now you can tell me while the clever ones are not listening ... what do you think of the Pickwick Papers ...

(MISS MATTY *looks up at this and catches* MISS POLE'S *eye* ... *Poor* MISS POLE *is caught between two fires.*)

MISS POLE (*nervously*). Well ... as to that, ma'am ...

(*But she is saved by* MR. HOGGINS *who has handed one tiny slice to each lady and has one piece of bread and butter left which he tenders to* MRS. JAMIESON.)

MR. H.   Now, Mrs. Jamieson... are you ready for another piece? See... this is the last slice and you know that means a handsome husband and a thousand a year... Who's going to be the lucky lady?

(MRS. JAMIESON *levels a withering glance at him.*)

MRS. J.   I do not appreciate your humour, sir...

LADY G.   A handsome husband and a thousand a year...! Nobody shall say I ever refused such an offer, Mr. Hoggins ... I will take it verra gladly...

(*The ladies lay down their cards and watch in silent horror as* MR. H. *crosses and hands the last slice to* LADY G. *with a deep bow and his hand on his heart...*)

Thank ye, sir...

MISS MATTY (*breaking the nervous tension, gives a deep sigh and a portentious shake of the head*).   Your bid, Mrs. Jamieson..

CURTAIN.

ACT TWO

Scene I

SCENE. *The same.*

TIME. *Late afternoon ... some months later.*

As the curtain rises, MRS. GASKELL *is revealed* D.L. *in front of the lowered gauze cloth.*

MRS. G. You know all about Cranford society now; you know all our weaknesses, and you know some of our virtues. You have seen that all of us, in some degree or other, are snobs; except perhaps Miss Matty ... but then she is a very exceptional person which is why this story is more about her than anybody else. You have heard also the first gentle footfall of progress, in the shape of Lady Glenmire.

(MARTHA *lights the candles on small table* L.C., *the lights fade in behind the gauze, and we see that the curtains are drawn and a small fire flickers in the hearth. A tea tray with only one cup on it is on the table ... we can see that somebody has finished tea.*)

This is the occasion of still another visit I paid to Miss Matty. But this time I came at the suggestion of Miss Pole, who wrote to me in great secrecy saying that she was a little worried about Miss Matty who has lately appeared to be sadly out of spirits ... and has even taken to lying down of an afternoon which is most unlike her. So I have taken it upon myself to propose a visit ... I have had my tea all alone, as you can see ... for Miss Matty as she told me ... spends her afternoons on her bed ...

(*Enter* MARY, *from* D.R. *She glances at the tea things.*)

MRS. G. There I am again ... (*She sighs.*) ... and very young ... but I am glad I remembered to use the back stairs and save wear on the front stair-carpet ...

(*Exit* MRS. GASKELL D.L. *The gauze cloth flies away.*)

MARTHA (*she is a little more civilized these days*). Oh... have you finished your tea, Miss Mary?
(*She hurries forward to take the tray.*)
MARY. Yes thank you, Martha... and I've just been up to see Miss Matty... she will be down presently...
MARTHA (*shaking her head*). Aye... she generally comes down about six... But it isn't like her, Miss, to spend every afternoon on her bed and miss her tea... it isn't like her at all...
MARY. Martha, tell me, how long has your mistress been so poorly...?
MARTHA (*laying down the tray again*). It was the first Tuesday after Christmas... in the evening, after Miss Pole had been, that she went into this moping way...
MARY. Quite suddenly...?
MARTHA. Yes. I thought she was tired that night and it would go off with a night's rest; but no!... she has gone on and on ever since till I thought it my duty to speak to Miss Pole and ask her to write to you...
MARY. You did quite right, Martha. And I hope you find your place comfortable...?
MARTHA (*moving* C.). Why, it seems so hard of missus not to let me have any followers...
MARY (*smiling*). Oh, is *that* all...?
MARTHA. There's such lots of young fellows in the town; and many a one has as much as offered to keep company with me... and I may never be in such a likely place again, and it's like wasting away my life...
MARY. Oh, I don't think it's as bad as all that, Martha...
MARTHA (*moving* D. R.). Take Miss Matty, now... all alone and off her food... If she'd taken that Mr. Holbrook when he was after her... she'd have a fine upstanding man about the house to care for her and put some body in her spirits...
MARY. That is enough about Mr. Holbrook and about your mistress, Martha...
MARTHA. I didn't mean to be impertinent, Miss... that's just how things looks to me... that's all...
MARY. *Very well*... that is all.

(MARY *moves to window.* MARTHA *picks up the tray again and is about to go out when we hear a soft knocking at the door* . . . *and presently* MISS POLE'S *voice* . . . *not as loud as usual* . . .)

MISS POLE (*off*). It is only I . . . Miss Pole . . .

(MARTHA *deposits the tray and approaches the door cautiously.*)

MARY. It's Miss Pole . . . let her in, Martha . . .

MARTHA (*we imagine she is peering through the letter box*). We have to be careful these days . . . there's been burglars in Cranford. . . . Ah . . . it's her all right . . .

(MARTHA *opens the door and* MISS POLE *darts quickly in* . . . *and* MARTHA *just as quickly shuts the door behind her.*)

MISS POLE. Thank you, Martha . . . you did quite right to take care . . . How are you, Mary, my dear?

(MARTHA *goes out to kitchen with tray.*)

MARY. How are you, Miss Pole . . . and what are all these precautions against robbers?

MISS POLE (*removing cloak and placing on table* U. R.). They say some very suspicious characters have been seen about of late . . . a man in a black cloak and a large moustache . . . But do not worry, my dear . . . we ladies of Cranford are more than a match for them. I would have come in to see you before but I knew Miss Matty would be resting and I did not want to disturb her . . .

MARY. It was kind of you to send for me, Miss Pole, and I am so glad you did . . .

MISS POLE (*below sofa*). Martha and I have been very worried about her. How do you think she looks?

MARY (*following* MISS P.). She certainly appears very low and does not take an interest in her food. Martha tells me this has been going on for more than two weeks . . .

MISS POLE (*sitting* L. *end of sofa*). About that . . . Let me see . . . it was the first Tuesday after Christmas that I dropped in after supper . . . I noticed she looked very down. I remember particularly because I came to tell her about the illness of Mr. Holbrook and I'd that moment heard it from Mr. Hoggins who was attending the poor man . . .

MARY (*crossing to fireplace*). Tell me about this Mr. Holbrook.
MISS POLE. Well, you see you would not have heard of him, my dear ... because it's more than fifteen years since he came to this house ... though he does live only a few miles out in the country ... does all his shopping in Misselton, they tell me ...
MARY (*lighting more candles*). He used to be a friend ... of ... of the Jenkyns family ... ?
MISS POLE (*making a decision*). I think I'd better tell you all about it, dear ... though it is very old gossip and there may be nothing in it ...
MARY. But you think this gentleman's illness is troubling Miss Matty?
MISS POLE. I'll not deny that I *have* been putting two and two together ... and you must remember this is all hearsay ...
                (MARY *nods and sits below fireplace.*)
But certain people say that Mr. Holbrook was very interested in Miss Matty and that he even offered for her ... and that she was ... well, she was not averse to his attentions. And then they say the Rector ... Miss Matty's father, invited him here to dinner one Sunday ... to look him over you know ... and that was the end of it.
MARY. But why ... ?
MISS POLE. Because Mr. Holbrook turned out to be not enough of a gentleman for the Jenkyns' family ... and so they sent him packing ...
MARY. Poor Miss Matty ... how cruel ... !
MISS POLE (*becoming very portentious*). But they do say ... that Mr. Holbrook behaved quite abominably ... so one could hardly blame the Rector ... (*She lowers her voice.*) You see, my dear, on the Sunday he came to dinner here ... they served green peas ... !
MARY. Yes ... ?
MISS POLE. And Mr. Holbrook ate them ... on his knife!
MARY. Poor Miss Matty ...
MISS POLE. So that, of course, was the end of that ... !

MARY. And all these years ... she has remembered him?
MISS POLE. Naturally nobody has ever mentioned the subject ... and I have never heard her speak his name ... but the very day I told her of his illness ... she went off her food and became sickly ....
MARY. But what are we to do ...?
MISS POLE (*in an explanatory manner*). We must guide the conversation, my dear, so that by the most delicate inference we show her how much happier a woman is if she avoids marriage ...
MARY. You think so ...?
MISS POLE. But we must be very subtle, of course ... perhaps you had better take your lead from me ... and remember, dear, be *subtle*—!
   (*There is a sound of a door opening and closing above.* MARY *glances apprehensively up and makes a warning sign* ... *She hastens to change the subject*...)
MARY (*in a slightly artificial voice*). And how is Lady Glenmire? Is she still in Cranford?
MISS POLE. No ... she left three weeks ago ... and Mrs. Jamieson is gone to Cheltenham to take the waters ...
MARY. And Lady Glenmire did not accompany her ...?
MISS POLE ... She went off somewhere else ... and I really could not say where for I never took a deal of interest in Lady Glenmire ... though some people were so impressed ...
MARY (*rising and moving* U. C.). I thought she was a nice. kindly woman ...
MISS POLE (*crossing to fireplace*). Kind enough, I daresay ... but not an idea of fashion in her head—
   (*Enter* MISS MATTY D.R. ... *She carries a candle* ...)
MISS MATTY (*moving* C.). Good evening, Miss Pole ...
MISS POLE. Good evening, Miss Matty ... and how are you today ...? I'm sure you'll cheer up now that you have dear Mary to stay with you again ...
MISS MATTY (*sits on sofa*). I'm sure I shall ... and indeed there is nothing whatever wrong with me ... It is just that I have not very much energy ..

MARY. I have told Martha that you are to take a raw egg in milk every morning.
MISS MATTY (*sits on* L. *end of sofa*). That is very kind of you, dear ... but that is enough about me ... I think I heard you discussing Lady Glenmire ...
MISS POLE. I was but remarking that she had no idea of fashion. She wore that same black dress the whole time she was here ...
MISS MATTY. But she is a widow ... so she must wear black ... and it was a very good silk for mourning—
MISS POLE (*sniffing*). Mourning ... Hmmmm. Then I must say that bombasine would have shown a deeper sense of her loss ...
MISS MATTY. We must remember, Miss Pole ... that her husband had been dead some years.
MISS POLE. That's as may be.
 (*There is a soft tapping at the door and the voice of* MISS BARKER.)
MISS B. (*off*). Do not be alarmed, ladies ... it is Miss Barker calling ...
MARY. Why does nobody use the doorbell?
MISS POLE. We have made a little arrangement among ourselves, dear ... Just to knock ... and to announce our names ... in that way we know it is a friend and not some robber ...
MARY (*rising to open the door*). I will let Miss Barker in ... no need to bother Martha ...
MISS MATTY. Thank you, Mary ... I think it is quite safe ... you see a stranger would be sure to ring the bell ...
 (MARY *opens the door to* MISS BARKER.)
MISS B. (*off*). Good evening, my dear, and how are you ...? Such a pleasure to welcome you to Cranford again ...
MARY (*off*). Very well, thank you, Miss Barker ... please come in ...
MISS B. (*entering and removing cloak and bonnet, coming down stage*). Good evening, ladies. I trust I do not intrude ...
MISS MATTY (*sitting on sofa*). We are very happy to see you, Miss Barker ... Please let Mary take your bonnet ...

(*The bonnet is removed and placed on a chair with her shawl.*)

MISS B. (*unctuous as ever*). I must not stay very long, Miss Jenkyns, for indeed I do not care to be out on the roads alone at night...

MISS MATTY. But stay for a little, Miss Barker, and tell us your news...

MISS B. (*sitting on sofa*). You are most kind, Miss Jenkyns, most kind; you pay me a great compliment in wishing to hear my news... but I fear that I have very little that could be of interest to you...

MISS MATTY (*nervously*). You have not chanced to hear about ...about that gentleman who is so ill... Mr. er...?

MISS B. (*unconscious of any importance in this question*). Mr. Holbrook, you mean? Oh... worse... much worse... they say he has not long to live...

MISS MATTY (*rising*). Oh... Oh... No... (*She jumps up.*) Such a strong light in here, it is quite trying to the eyes... you will excuse me if I move these candles...

(*She turns her back on the company and makes a great business of moving the candles from small table to window table.* MARY *and* MISS POLE *frown and shake their heads at* MISS B. *who fails to get the point and continues.*)

MISS B. And a great pity it is for a finer man I never saw... though it is some years since I set eyes on him... but I remember he was a very handsome man... Do you not remember, Miss Pole...?

MISS POLE (*sitting on sofa, trying to change the subject*). I was just speaking of Lady Glenmire when you came, Miss Barker...

MARY (*moving to* L. *end of sofa, eagerly*). Oh yes, tell me, Miss Barker... what did you think of Lady Glenmire...?

MISS MATTY (*timorously*). But I suppose there is a chance ...they tell me there is always a *chance*... that he... a patient, that is... can recover...?

MISS B. Mr. Holbrook? Oh... I suppose there is always a chance... but we shall hear this evening, no doubt, for I saw Mr. Hoggins this afternoon getting into his gig in a great hurry ... Mr. Holbrook's housekeeper had sent for him ... and he asked me to tell you he would be by later for the St. James's Chronicle as today is Thursday ... if he could get away, that is ...

MISS MATTY. If he could get away ... ?

MISS B. From Mr. Holbrook ... For of course he would not leave before the end ...

MARY. But, Miss Barker ... very likely Mr. Hoggins will be able to help ... the ... the patient ... and perhaps he will bring us news that he is quite recovered ...

MISS POLE (*very lightly*). Certainly ... depend on it ... I am sure we shall hear that the poor man is quite recovered.

MISS MATTY (*moving to* C.). Do you think so, Miss Pole? ... You are always so clever about these things.

MISS POLE. I haven't a doubt in the world ...

MARY. Do sit down, dear Miss Matty ... I am so anxious to hear what Miss Barker thinks of Lady Glenmire ...

(MISS MATTY *seats herself carefully with her back to the light.*)

MISS POLE (*nodding knowingly at* MARY). I was just saying that Cranford could get along very well without her ... ladyship ...

MISS MATTY. I liked her ... she was so straightforward ... and so simple ...

MISS POLE (*triumphantly*). Exactly! Simple is the word ... and to my mind there is not much difference between being simple ... and downright silly ...

MISS B. (*always impressed by the title*). I do not think I should care to call a member of our nobility silly ...

MISS POLE (*with a meaning look at* MARY). I have had a good deal of experience in my life, and I have remarked that *any* woman who is *unable* to keep herself from getting married is no more nor less than *simple* ... !

MISS B. How thankful we should all be that we ladies of Cranford are safe from it ...

MISS POLE (*who does not care to be considered all that "safe," crossing to fire*). Safe! I do not know what you mean, Miss Barker; we are *none* of us safe as long as there is a man alive to try to lead us on with his lies and the like. And I, for one, shall never cease to be upon my guard...

MISS B. Oh, how right you are, Miss Pole... I only meant how lucky we are that there are no unmarried men in Cranford... except Mr. Hoggins and the Vicar...

MISS POLE. And even *vicars* are not always to be trusted...

MISS MATTY. But our vicar is such a nice man... and so considerate...

MISS POLE. There you are you see... That is one of their little games... they'll always pretend to be considerate... Mark my words, Mary...

MARY. I certainly will remember what you say, Miss Pole...

MISS POLE. And do you not agree that is very good advice for a young girl, Miss Matty?

MISS MATTY. Well... I may say there was a time when I thought I should not have been only Miss Matty Jenkyns all my life...

MISS POLE. Then, I'm sure Miss Matty, that you should be very thankful. And as for your dead sister... she was always a champion of the unmarried state...

MISS MATTY. ... I remember when we were girls... she told me once that she would like to marry an archdeacon... and write his sermons...

MISS B. A very high-minded ambition... but I am sure she was thankful she never did...

MISS MATTY. She never met an unmarried archdeacon in her life...

MISS POLE (*devoutly*). Providence was kind.

MISS MATTY (*rising, crossing to window*). If you will excuse me... I was thinking of making some spills... I have a box of old letters and bills here... (*She brings the box back to the circle of ladies.*) Perhaps you would be kind enough to help me... (*She takes them to sofa.*)

MISS B. A pleasure...

MARY. Of course, Miss Matty...

MISS MATTY. We will start with the bills...

(*Each lady takes a piece of paper and starts to roll a spill*

... *which is a small tube of paper used for the lighting of candles.*)

MISS POLE. Such a saving in matches...

MISS MATTY (*with assumed casualness*). Mr. Hoggins did not say at what time he expected...to...to call for the Chronicle...?

MISS B. That of course will depend on...

MARY (*quickly*). Let us see who can make the most spills in the shortest time...

MISS POLE. A capital idea...Hurry, Miss Barker...or I shall beat you...

(*They each dive into the box and seize a paper which they start to roll with great energy.* MISS BARKER *comes out with a bundle of faded letters tied with a ribbon...*)

MISS B. Why...I have some letters tied up with ribbon... they look almost like *billets-doux*...

MISS MATTY (*very calmly taking them from her*). I think I will not destroy those...yet. (*She places them on the mantel.*)

(*There is a ring at the doorbell. They all start up.*)

MISS POLE. The bell...it must be a stranger...!

MISS MATTY. Perhaps it is Mr. Hoggins...

(*Enter* MARTHA *from kitchen.*)

All right, Martha...I feel sure it is but Mr. Hoggins... I will open the door myself...

MARTHA. Yes, ma'am...

(*Exit* MARTHA. MISS MATTY, *who is always at her best in times of stress...goes directly to the door without a tremour...and opens it...Enter* MR. HOGGINS.)

MR. H. (*off*). Good evening, ma'am. If it is not too late, I have come for my Chronicle...

MISS MATTY (*moving* D. L.). Come in, Mr. Hoggins. I have it here for you on the table...

MR. H. (*moving* C., *coming downstage*). Good evening, ladies... (*They all bob politely but nobody has the courage to speak.*)

I am a little late to call...but I have been with a patient all afternoon...poor man...

(*There is still dead silence.*)

And I am leaving on the early train tomorrow ... and shall be away for a few days ...

(*Silence. At last* MISS MATTY, *without the slightest quiver in her voice ... and with complete calm ... perhaps too much for* MISS MATTY ... *speaks* ...)

MISS MATTY. And your ... patient, sir? He will not need you ... ?

MR. H. Mr. Holbrook? No, he will not be needing me again ... he died, ma'am, a short while ago ... God rest his soul.

MISS MATTY. Yes ... yes ... God rest his soul ...

(*There is a slight pause and then she continues very firmly.*) (*Moving* U.C.) If you will excuse me, please ... I must go upstairs ... Good evening, Miss Pole ... Miss Barker ... Mr. Hoggins ...

(*She takes the packet of letters, curtseys slightly and mounts the stairs quite calmly. Exit* MISS MATTY.)

MISS POLE (*moving* U. L.). Come along, Miss Barker ... it is time we were going ...

(*She collects her bonnet and shawl from the chair.*)

MR. H. Miss Matty was not offended that I called so late ...?

MARY. No ... no, of course not ... I think she has one of her headaches ... they come on very suddenly ...

MISS B. (*adjusting her bonnet*). And will you be away from Cranford for long, Mr. Hoggins ... ?

MR. H. A week at the most ... I cannot stay longer away. I was to have left a week ago ... but poor Holbrook was so ill ...

MISS POLE (*with many a knowing nod to* MARY). Come, Miss Barker ... and Mr. Hoggins, perhaps you will give us the benefit of your company ... the roads are so dark ... and with all these robberies going on ...

MR. H. A pleasure, ma'am ... though there's no such thing as a robber in Cranford ... but any excuse to escort two ladies ... Good night to you, Miss Mary ...

(*They all go out with a chorus of "Good nights".*)

MR. H. Am I not a lucky man to have two such companions . . . ?
   (*They are out of sight when* MISS POLE *pops her head back in . . .*)
MISS POLE. You see what I mean, Mary, about men . . . Thank goodness I have Miss Barker with me . . . (*Exit . . .*)
   (MARY *comes back down stage looking very thoughtful . . . She commences absently to role a spill . . . Then* MISS MATTY *creeps back down the stairs . . . carrying the packet of letters.*)
MISS MATTY. Have they gone, dear?
MARY. Yes, Miss Matty . . . do sit down . . . are you quite all right . . . ?
MISS MATTY (*moving to fire*). Thank you, yes, dear, I am quite all right . . . Just one of my headaches . . . I think perhaps I will burn these after all . . .
MARY. You would not like to read them first . . . ?
MISS MATTY. No dear . . . I think it is sometimes better not to indulge oneself in fancies . . . sentimental fancies from the past . . .
   (*She drops the packet into the fire and watches for a moment as the flames spring up and die away again.*)
MARY (*trying to be very bright*). Miss Matty . . . I brought a fashion paper for you . . . from Drumble . . . It has pictures of the very latest caps and bonnets . . . Do let me show it to you . . .
   (MARY *produces the paper from a side table.*)
MARY (*sitting on sofa* L. *end*). See . . . the models are quite new . . .
MISS MATTY (*sitting on sofa* R. *end, glancing at it with little interest*). I was thinking . . . that when I have a new cap, I should like one like Mrs. Jamieson's . . .
MARY (*thoughtlessly*). But Mrs. Jamieson wears a *widow's* cap . . . (*She stops suddenly.*)
MISS MATTY. Oh . . . but I only meant something similar . . .
MARY. Oh . . . of course . . .

MISS MATTY. I have been thinking, dear, that I should give you a little advice, I should not like you to be frightened by Miss Pole from being married. And if ever a gentleman should please you very much, and should propose, I do not think it would be silly to accept him. And even if Miss Pole is right and it is only credulous ladies who get married, I think perhaps a little credulity might help one through life very smoothly...

MARY. Perhaps you are right, Miss Matty...

MISS MATTY. And perhaps being over credulous is better than doubting and doubting and seeing difficulties and disagreeables in everything...

MARY. I am sure it is, Miss Matty...

MISS MATTY. Then I want you to promise me, dear... that should you meet a gentleman that well... that you like... and if he should... if it should be reciprocated...

MARY. I understand, Miss Matty...

MISS MATTY. No dear... I have not finished yet. I want you to promise that if this gentleman proposes, you will not lightly turn him down... or let others persuade you against him... Other people can hold such unimportant things against a person... such silly things... like, like table manners... for instance...

MARY. I promise, Miss Matty...

MISS MATTY. And you would not hold it against a gentleman if he should do something unimportant such as—well, eat green peas with his knife...?

MARY. I would not care how he should eat his peas...

MISS MATTY. And for that matter... though this is all nonsense, of course... I have been told that some very nice people eat their green peas with a knife...

MARY. I believe in some parts of the country it is quite the accepted thing...

MISS MATTY (*happily, moving* C.). Is that so, dear... I am very happy to hear you say so...

(*Enter* MARTHA *from kitchen.*)

MARTHA. Will you be wanting anything more tonight, ma'am...?

MISS MATTY. No thank you... goodnight, Martha...
MARTHA. Goodnight, ma'am... goodnight, Miss....
MISS MATTY. Just a minute, Martha... I...
    (MARTHA *returns and stands expectantly.*)
  Martha! You are very young...
    (*Another long pause.*)
MARTHA. Yes, please, ma'am; two and twenty last third of October, please, ma'am.
MISS MATTY. And perhaps, Martha, you may some time meet with a young man you like, and who likes you...
MARTHA (*radiant*). Oh, yes... ma'am!
MISS MATTY. Now, I did say you were not to have followers; but if you meet with such a young man, and tell me, and I find he is respectable... I have no objection to his coming to see you once a week...
MARTHA (*ecstatically*). Oh... Thank you, ma'am... thank you...
    (*And she turns on her heels and literally tears to the kitchen door.* Exit MARTHA.)
MISS MATTY. Bless my soul... How very remarkable...
    (*Suddenly there is a commotion in the kitchen... and in a moment* MARTHA *enters dragging a tall handsome young man... A bit rough and very shy... It is* JEM HEARN.)
MARTHA. Please ma'am, here's Jem Hearn... and he's a joiner making three and sixpence a day, and six foot one in his stocking feet, and if you'll ask about him tomorrow, everyone will give him a character for steadiness... and he'll be glad enough to call any night, *I'll be bound*...!

CURTAIN.

ACT TWO
SCENE II

SCENE. *The same.*

TIME. *About eight o'clock... of an evening a week or so later.*

(At RISE: *Curtains are drawn... candles lighted and fire burning.* MISS MATTY, MISS POLE... MISS BARKER *and* MRS. FORRESTER *are sitting at the card table... very intent upon their game of preference.* MARY *sits by the fire, busy with needlework. Since the ladies of Cranford have only two dresses, one for the morning, and one for the afternoon, we see that the only change in their appearance is in their caps... different degrees of elaboration in which signify varying grades of importance of the occasion.* MISS MATTY *is wearing a new cap... A very observant person might note that it bears a strong resemblance to that widow's cap which* MRS. JAMIESON *wore.*

Enter MARTHA *bearing the silver tray with five small cups.* MISS MATTY *looks up in astonishment...*)

MISS MATTY (*rising and crossing to table behind sofa*). Oh... Martha... the ptisan already... how quickly the time has flown...!

MARTHA (*who appears strangely agitated*). It's eight o'clock...

MISS MATTY. A little lemon-verbena ptisan, ladies, to keep you warm on the way home.

MISS B. How excessively thoughtful...

(MARTHA *deposits the tray and* MARY *rises to hand round the cups.*)

MISS POLE (*totting up the score-card*). I declare!... Ladies, I am afraid I am the winner...

MRS. F. (*accepting a cup from* MARY). Delicious...

MISS POLE. That will be tuppence from each of you, if you please...

(*They each count out two pennies.*)
MISS MATTY. You may take the tray now, Martha... and leave the cups... (*She turns to the ladies.*) With these robbers about, I don't feel happy till the silver is safe under my bed...
MRS. F. (*nervously*). There haven't been any *more* robberies... have there...?
MARTHA (*moving* C., *joining in eagerly*). I just heard, ma'am ... there's been a terrible thing this very evening... Mrs. Deacon stopped at the back door to warn us...
(*There is a chorus of squeaks of alarm.*)
MISS MATTY. What is it, Martha... what has happened...?
MARTHA (*moving* U.C.). Well, it seems that Mr. Hoggins came back this evening... he's been away for a week or so as you know... and just as he was about to ring his own front door-bell... two masked men... horrible looking men, they was...
MRS. F. (*almost fainting*). I can't bear it...
MISS POLE. Calm yourself, Mrs. Forrester...
MARTHA. With great big faces and great big whiskers...
MISS B. (*almost screaming*). Whiskers...!
MISS MATTY. Go on, Martha... go on...
MARTHA. And terrible staring eyes...
MARY (*moving to* L. *below* C.). And what did these men do, Martha?
MARTHA. Set on him... something horrible...
MISS POLE. And did they rob him...?
MARTHA. Took everything he had... and his clothes too ... left him without a stitch... naked, he was...
MISS MATTY (*terribly shocked*). Martha! You must not use that word... it is not proper...
MARTHA. No, ma'am... but there he was in his birthday suit... a knocking at his door... and the men, they ran off up the road...
MRS. F. (*breathlessly*). Oh dear... they are still at large...
MISS B. (*very shrill*). And we have to go home in the *dark!*
MISS POLE. I knew this would happen... I am sure they are the very men I saw the other day... Did one of them have

a cast in his eye?

MARTHA. Oh... a terrible squint...

(*More squeaks of alarm which continue during this conversation.*)

MISS POLE. And another one with a hunched back?

MARTHA. That's it... a great, enormous hump sprouting out of his shoulders...

MISS POLE. And greasy black hair hanging down over his forehead...?

MARTHA. And hanging right down his back.....!

MISS POLE (*nodding triumphantly*). The very same gang I spoke about to Mr. Hoggins himself before he went away... and he laughed at me... mind you... laughed at me...! You remember, Miss Barker? The night he escorted us home...?

MISS B. I do... indeed I do... And we have to go home in the *dark*...

MISS MATTY. You must both spend the night here... and we will barricade the doors... Miss Pole only lives just across the back gardens so I daresay she will be safe...

MISS POLE (*rather taken aback*). Yes... yes of course...

MARY. What time is Jem due back from Missleton, Martha?

MARTHA. He ought to be back any time now... he said he'd look in... just to... just to say good night...

MARY. Jem is Martha's young man... and when he calls I am sure he would not mind escorting you ladies home...

MISS MATTY (*with relief*). Of course... and he is very big and strong...

MARTHA. Very strong.

MISS POLE. Then, to be on the safe side... I think we should accept the offer, ladies... not that I personally have the slightest fear, of course...

MRS. F. You are sure he is very strong...?

MARTHA. He'd be a match for ten men... would Jem...

MISS B. Will he be very late, do you think...?

MARTHA. He said he'd be here before nine...

MRS. F. And you are certain he will call...?

MARTHA. He'll call all right ... on account of he's got a very special ... reason ...
MISS MATTY. Jem has gone to Missleton today to buy the engagement ring ... !
MISS B. Indeed ... what a fortunate girl you are, Martha.
MISS POLE. Remember, Martha, that a ring is the symbol of a woman's bondage !
MARTHA. That's just what I think, ma'am ... and a girl can't feel safe until she's got one ... !
MISS MATTY. You may take the tray now, Martha, and put it under the bed ...

(MARTHA *picks up the tray and makes for the stairs ... but* MISS POLE *cannot let well alone.*)

MISS POLE (*moving to* MARTHA). I said bondage, Martha ... and that means you are bound to a *man* for *life* ... !
MARTHA (*happily*). That's the way of it, Miss Pole ... and what I say is, there's nothing like a bit o' bondage to keep you warm ...

(*Exit* MARTHA *upstairs.*)
(MISS P. *sits on* L. *end of sofa.*)

MISS MATTY. Poor Mr. Hoggins ... I hope he was not severely wounded ... and I did not know he had even returned from his holiday ...

(*They abandon the card-table and draw their chairs nervously round the fire.*)

MRS. F. And to think that such a thing could happen in Cranford ... and in the centre of the town, too ... right on his doorstep ...
MISS B. Yes, and if such a brutal assault can take place here in the town, only think of the dangers Mrs. Forrester must face on her way home ... for she lives more than a hundred yards up Darkness Lane ...
MRS. F. (*terrified again*). Darkness Lane ... ! Oh dear ... !
(MARY *sits on sofa.*)
MISS POLE (*taking charge*). No ladies, we must not become hysterical ... Remember, Mrs. Forrester, your father was a soldier ... and so was mine. And I'll warrant that we women could outwit a few poor, simple men any day in the week ...

Mrs. F. But only think what horrid brutes they must be... all covered with whiskers.
Miss B. I declare I should die if I even saw such monsters... surely they cannot be *English*...?
Miss Pole. Of course they are not English... it is a gang... that is what it is... a foreign gang...
Mrs. F. Probably spies...
Miss Matty. Spies! Oh dear me... but what could they spy upon in Cranford?
Miss Pole (*darkly*). Ha! You never know... with foreigners...
Mrs. F. My father always said that the French were a nation of spies... it is probably the French... a French gang...
Mary. But remember Jem will be here to take you home and I assure you he is very strong...
Miss Pole. Of course... and everybody knows that *one* Englishman is worth *ten* of any other race... my father said so frequently...
Miss Matty. So I have often heard... and yet your father fought in America... and the Americans won the war...
Miss Pole. Pure chance...!
Miss Matty. I suppose so.
Mary. Listen...! Someone is coming up the path... I can hear voices...!
    (*That all jump to their feet in violent alarm.*)
Miss Pole (*seizing the poker*). Courage, ladies...!
    (Mary *picks up fire irons and each takes one... The tongs, the shovel, the brushes, etc.* Martha *comes running down the stairs...*)
Martha. There's folks in the front garden...
Mrs. F. (*sinking back on sofa*). I am sorry, ladies... but I cannot... I cannot...
Miss Matty (*taking her weapon from her so that she now has two*). Never mind, Mrs. Forrester... Miss Pole is in charge...
Miss Pole (*not so sure of herself now*). Yes... yes... Now... we must be calm at all costs...
Mary. I will look out of the window...

MISS MATTY. Just a minute, Mary dear ... (*She darts into the hall and returns with a soldier's hat of the Waterloo period.*) It was my grandfather's ... I brought it down the other day ... just in case ... if they see your head at the window they will think it is a man and run away——

MISS POLE (*moving* C.). I think it would be safer to look from an upper window ... Allow me ... (*She takes the hat and advances to stairs ... putting it on ...*) I will reconnoitre from above. Meanwhile, ladies ... Courage ... !

(*Exit* MISS POLE *upstairs.*)

MISS MATTY. Oh dear ... how brave of her ... !

MISS B. But now we are all alone ... !

MRS. F. (*weakly*). Water ... !

(*There is a sudden loud knock at the door ... A chorus of frightened squeaks from the ladies ...* MARY *advances uncertainly to the door.*)

MISS MATTY (*suddenly calm and dignified, as always in an emergency*). No, Mary ... This is *my* duty ... Stand back, please ...

MARY. But, Miss Matty ...

MISS MATTY. No, Mary ... I shall tell them that I am the Rector's daughter ... and a Jenkyns ... !

MARTHA. Let me, ma'am ... I've got a good right arm.

MISS MATTY. No, Martha ... stand back, please ...

(*She approaches the door, flanked by* MARY *and* MARTHA.)

MISS B. Magnificent! ... a true Jenkyns ... !

MISS MATTY (*opening the letter-box and calling through it*). Who goes there? Stand back ... or I fire ... !

(*We hear a voice from without ... It is the voice of* MR. HOGGINS.)

MR. H. (*off*). It's only me, ma'am ... Hoggins ...

(*There is a short pause in which they all begin to feel very silly.*)

Mr. Hoggins ... at your service, ma'am ...

MISS MATTY. Oh ... just a minute, Mr. Hoggins ... (*She unbolts the door ... and opens it just a crack.*) Dear Mr. Hoggins ... come in at once ...

(MR. HOGGINS *squeezes in and they quickly fasten the*

door behind him... Ad libs of "Mr. Hoggins"—"Poor Mr. Hoggins" etc.... from all.)

MR. H. Good evening to you, ladies...

(*But they give him no time to finish a sentence... They crowd solicitously round him... jabbering away like so many magpies...*)

MISS MATTY. Poor Mr. Hoggins, are you seriously hurt? How brave of you to come out again...

MR. H. (*looking back at the door*). But, Madam... I do not understand... you shut the door in...

MARTHA. Don't you worry, sir... they won't get in here...

MR. H. But the door... there is someone outside...!

MISS MATTY. Were you followed...? Is it the gang...?

MR. H. Ladies... please... What *is* all this about?

MARY. The robbers, Mr. Hoggins... the men that attacked you...

MR. H. Nobody has attacked me, ladies...

MISS MATTY. But we heard you had been set upon...

MR. H. Then you were misinformed... I only returned from London this evening and...

MISS B. But on your doorstep... we heard you were savagely attacked... that they were lurking by the porch.

(*She sits on L. end of sofa.*)

MR. H. Once and for all, ladies... *nobody* has lurked in my porch... and *nobody* has attacked me... I am very well, and only call upon you so late because I have some very pleasant news for you...

MISS MATTY (*reproachfully*). Martha...!

MARTHA (*who is just disappearing into the kitchen*). That Mrs. Deacon always did exaggerate a bit...

MR. H. And now, Miss Jenkyns... may I open the door? For it was shut in the face of somebody who wishes to see you...

(*The ladies return their weapons to the hearth rather self-consciously.*)

MISS MATTY. Of course... of course... I am so very sorry, Mr. Hoggins... Who can it be...?

MR. H. (*going to the door*). The person who is waiting outside, ladies ... is someone I am very eager to present to you ... for it is none other than my *wife!*
(*Ad libs of "wife"!*)
Yes, ladies ... I am a bachelor no longer ... for I was married a week ago in London ... And now ...
(MARY *collects the fire irons and replaces them in the grate. He opens the door and in steps* LADY GLENMIRE.)
MISS MATTY. Lady Glenmire ... !
MISS B. (*rising*). ⎧Your Ladyship ... !
MRS. F. (*rising*). ⎩Bless my soul ... !
MISS MATTY. Come in, Lady Glenmire ... but, Mr. Hoggins, just was saying ... (*She pauses in bewilderment.*)
LADY G. No ... Miss Jenkyns ... not Lady Glenmire ... Mrs. Hoggins!
MISS MATTY. Mrs. Hoggins! I can hardly believe it ... ! I hope you will be very happy ... very happy, indeed ... I'm sure ... I must congratulate you, Mr. Hoggins ... !
MR. H. Thank you, ma'am ... I'm a very lucky man ...
MISS B. My very best wishes ... your ... ma'am ... A great surprise, I'm sure ... !
(*She sits.*)
MRS. F. Indeed, a surprise ...
MRS. H. Thank ye, ladies ... Thank ye ... Ye're all verra kind. I could not wait to come and tell ye ... for I knew ye would wish me well ...
(*Enter* MISS POLE *very sheepishly down stairs ... She tries to appear casual but has forgotten to remove the hat.*)
MR. H. Why ... if it isn't Miss Pole ... and wearing another new head-dress ... !
(MISS POLE *snatches off the hat.*)
MRS. H. Good evening to ye, Miss Pole ... and are we just in time for charades?
MISS MATTY. Miss Pole ... Mr. Hoggins has just this minute announced his marriage ... to Lady Glenmire ...
MISS POLE (*rather coldly*). I overhead ... on the stairs. Allow me to congratulate you, *Mrs. Hoggins* ...
MRS. H. That is verra kind, Miss Pole. I declare I was almost

afraid to face all you ladies for fear ye'd be angry with me for taking Mr. Hoggins out of the market...

MISS POLE (*becoming very sharp*). Do not apologize, madam ... for the ladies of Cranford have *other* things to think about than marriage...

(*She moves to the fireplace.*)

MR. H. Yes, indeed... and this evening they have all been in a sad fright, thinking about robbers...

MISS MATTY. Oh yes... we were very alarmed, for we heard that Mr. Hoggins had been set upon and robbed...

MR. H. It has all grown out of the fact, no doubt, that while I was in London a cat broke into my larder and stole a leg of mutton...

MISS B. But Miss Pole herself has seen a gang of men skulking about...

MRS. F. With whiskers... I

MR. H. Then if you are still alarmed, ladies... Mrs. Hoggins and myself will be delighted to escort you home...

MRS. F. Thank you... it is very kind... (*Rising.*) I think I will accept... just in case...

MISS B. I think perhaps I will too... (*Rising.*) if you don't mind...

MRS. H. (MISS MATTY *pulls the bell rope*). That's the way... it's a fine, clear night... and the extra walk will do us good... We'll be getting along now... I only wanted to tell Miss Jenkyns our news before she heard it from another party...

(*Enter* MARTHA.)

MISS MATTY (*moving* D. L.). The ladies are leaving, Martha... their cloaks, please...

(MARTHA, MISS BARKER *and* MRS. FORRESTER *go out to the hall for their cloaks.*)

MR. H. (*moving to* MISS M.). While I was in London I heard some bad news about our local railway... it seems they are going bankrupt...

MISS MATTY. I'm not surprised... what else can you expect from such a dirty, dangerous thing... as a railway—?

MR. H. Maybe... but the Town and County Bank hold most of the shares... it'll be a bad thing for some of the folks hereabouts . . . for the Bank will go too . . .

MISS MATTY. Oh . . . you need have no fear if it is the Town and County Bank . . . for my sister, who was very clever about such things . . . had the highest opinion of it . . . and she was always right about financial matters . . .

(MRS. HOGGINS *moves* C. *and* MRS. F. *and* MISS B. *return wearing cloaks, etc.*)

MR. H. Just the same madam . . . I am glad I am not a shareholder . . . Well . . . are we ready, ladies? Miss Pole . . . ?

MISS POLE. No thank you, sir . . . I am not afraid to go home alone.

MR. H. With all those men about . . . covered with whiskers?

MISS POLE (*meaningly*). I have yet to meet the man, with or without whiskers, who could get the better of *me*!

MRS. H. Then we'll be away . . . and a good night to you all . . .

MRS. F. (*off*). Good night, Miss Matty . . . such a relief . . .

MISS B. (*off*). Good night . . . such an eventful evening . . . !

MISS MATTY. Good night . . .

(MARTHA *holds open the door and* MR. *and* MRS. H., MISS B., *and* MRS. F. *go out. The moment the door is closed* MISS POLE *literally bursts into speech.*)

MISS POLE. Well . . . ! Did you ever hear the like of it . . . ? And the deception of it . . . !

MISS MATTY (*mildly, moving to sofa*). Oh . . . I think they are very well suited . . .

(*She sits.*)

MISS POLE. Creeping off to London like that, to get themselves married . . . as if they were ashamed of it . . .

MISS MATTY. She was a widow . . . and I expect she preferred a quiet wedding somewhere . . .

MISS POLE. Very likely. And that leg of mutton . . . stolen by a cat . . . I never heard such a stupid story. I believe he was robbed just like Martha told us, and is ashamed to own it . . .

MARY. But I do not see why he should be ashamed . . .

MISS POLE. Because you do not know men, my dear; depend upon it, he is ashamed to admit he was set upon and over-

powered... by three mere Frenchmen—
MISS MATTY. Then you think the robbers are still at large...?
MISS POLE. Not a doubt of it... Did I not see them with my own eyes...?
MISS MATTY. Oh dear... I would have preferred to believe Mr. Hoggins...
MISS POLE (*moving to door*). Now I must go. My calash please, Martha...
MISS MATTY. But if they are still about... are you not afraid...?
MISS POLE. I...? Afraid...? (*She returns* C.). But if I were you, Miss Matty, I should lock up the house very safely ...just as well to keep up our precautions in spite of what my Lady Hoggins may have to say about her leg of mutton ...I wonder what Mrs. Jamieson will have to say about my lady's marriage... *she* won't receive them in *her* house... I'm sure of that...
MISS MATTY. Oh dear... perhaps she will not expect us to receive them either...
MARY. I expect she is very fond of Mrs. Hoggins... She surely could not object to her marriage—
MISS POLE. Hmmm. Well, good night. I shall reserve my judgment until Mrs. Jamieson's return... until then... Mr. and Mrs. Hoggins certainly exist... but the less said about them, the better... like the Queen of Spain's legs—
    (*Exit* MISS POLE. MARTHA *closes the door behind her and returns* D. C.)
MISS MATTY. And now, Martha... I'm sure Jem will not be coming tonight... so we must lock up... I think we will take the usual precautions... as Miss Pole says...
MARTHA. Fire irons...?
MISS MATTY. Yes... I will attend to the front door... and you can see to the back...
    (*Exit* MARTHA. MISS MATTY *collects all the fire irons from the hearth and carries them to the front door where she stacks them.*)
MISS MATTY. A little idea of mine, Mary dear... you see if we stack them like this... and someone should force the

door... the irons will fall... and we shall hear them...
(*She goes off to front door.*)
MARY. Yes... and what do we do then...?
MISS MATTY (*returning*). I prefer not to think beyond that point, my dear... and you will oblige me by not mentioning it so late at night... And now for the candles... (*She takes up a candelabrum from table* L.) Martha and I make it a point to make a small tour of inspection before retiring...
(*Enter* MARTHA *from* D.R.)
Everything safe in the kitchen, Martha...? The fire irons against the door...?
MARTHA. Yes, ma'am, and the coal bucket.
MISS MATTY. Very good. Now we will just inspect the bedrooms...
(*They are half way up the stairs when there is a terrific knocking at the front door...* MISS POLE'S *voice is heard in violent alarm...*)
(*They return down stairs.*)
MISS POLE. It is Miss Pole... let me in... Miss Matty... let me in...!
(MARY *and* MARTHA *to above sofa.*)
MISS MATTY (*wrestling with the irons and opening the door.*) Dear me... Miss Pole... I hope she has not been assaulted...
(*Enter* MISS POLE *carrying a large basket covered with a cloth...*)
MISS POLE (*handing the basket to* MARY). Take care of that... it's my silver...
(*She sinks into sofa quite out of breath.* MARTHA *and* MARY *to* R. *of sofa.*)
MISS MATTY. Dear Miss Pole... Have you been attacked?
MISS POLE. I was too quick for them... but I was *followed!*
MARY. By whom... the men...?
MISS POLE. The gang...
MISS MATTY. How terrible! Tell us all about it, Miss Pole... Martha! The fire irons...
(MARTHA *re-stacks the irons at the door.*)
MISS POLE. Well, it was like this... when I got home I

found a note from my Betty saying Mrs. Deacon had called and told her about the robbers so she was gone to spend the night with her mother ... And then ...

MISS MATTY. Yes ... then ... ?

MISS POLE. Then I heard footsteps ... stealthy footsteps ... so I bundled my silver together in that basket ... and decided I would spend the night with you ... just a precaution, of course ...

MISS MATTY. How wise of you, Miss Pole ...

MISS POLE. But the worst of all ... is that as I was coming up the road ... I was *followed* ... by an enormous man. However, I have always had great presence of mind, as you know ...

MISS MATTY. Of course ... So what did you do ... ?

MISS POLE. I ran.

MARY (*also getting nervous now*). Then he saw you come into this house with your silver ... ?

MISS MATTY. Oh dear ... then they will attack this house next ... Take Miss Pole's silver, Mary, and put it under the bed ...

MISS POLE. I hope I have not attracted the danger to your house, Miss Matty ...

MISS MATTY. Not at all ... If we have to be murdered, it is better to be murdered all together ...

MISS POLE. Naturally ... I will take charge again in case of emergency ...

(*There is a sudden and deafening crash from the kitchen ... They are all paralysed ...*)

(*All run* L.)

MISS MATTY. It's the kitchen fire irons ... !

MISS POLE. They are attacking in the rear ... !

MARY. Listen ... !

MISS MATTY. Footsteps ... !

(*And indeed there are footsteps, heavy, cautious footsteps in the kitchen. The ladies draw together in a tight little knot. The footsteps continue ... They stumble but go on ... Then very slowly, and with a hideous squeak, the kitchen door opens ... And in comes* JEM. *He stands blinking in the light.*)

MARTHA (*moving* D. R.). Jem! Jem, you big oaf...!
MISS MATTY (*moving* C.). Oh... Jem... we thought you were a robber... How did you get in...?
MARTHA (*moving* D. R.). I put the fire irons agin the door...
(MISS P. *breaks* D. L.)
JEM (*rubbing a shin*). That you did, lass... but you didn't lock it...
MISS POLE. Fancy walking into a respectable house at this time of night!
JEM (*moving* C.) I knows it's a bit late, ma'am... but I saw the lights on... and I see'd you a walkin' up the path ma'am ... and I was a goin' to ask if it was too late ma'am... when you took to your 'eels and run...
MARY (*with relief*). So it was only Jem, Miss Pole, who followed you...
MISS MATTY. Well, never mind now... but it is late Jem, so give Martha the engagement ring and then you must go...
JEM (*turning to* MARTHA). Well... you see... it's like this... I didn't get no ring...
MARTHA (*very sharply*). Then you been long enough, I must say... gettin' nothing...
JEM (*in great distress*). There, lass... I chose your ring all right... Only when it come to pay for it...
MARTHA. You'd already drunk up your five pun note, I daresay... you good-for-nothin'...
JEM (*appealingly to* MISS MATTY). If you could keep 'er quiet a minute, ma'am...?
MISS MATTY. Now, Martha... do not get excited... let Jem tell us all about it...
JEM. Thank you, ma'am. Well... like I said I picked a ring ... and then I come to pay for it and I give him a five pun note... and he looks at it... and says it ain't no good and it's only paper... which I could see... only I got paid with that note... and they tells me paper's as good as money... only now it seems it ain't any more... and that's part of my savings, ma'am... and I don't rightly understand... and mayhap you could explain... and stop

fidgetting, Martha . . .

MISS MATTY. He told you the bank note was worthless . . . ?

MISS POLE. That would be the bank Mr. Hoggins was talking about . . .

MISS MATTY. What bank was it, Jem . . . ? I mean what bank does your note belong to . . . ?

JEM (*producing it*). It says "Town and County Bank" . . .

MISS MATTY. Let me see it . . . (*She takes it.*) Yes, this is the bank Mr. Hoggins mentioned . . .

MISS POLE. It has gone bankrupt, Jem . . . that means they haven't any money . . .

MISS MATTY (*quite proudly*). The Town and County Bank is *my* bank . . . My sister, who was very wise about such things, put all our money in it . . . that means that I am a shareholder.

MARY (*in great alarm*). All . . . your money, Miss Matty . . . ?

MISS MATTY. Yes, dear. And Jem, as I am a shareholder, it is my duty to re-imburse you the full value of this note . . . Hand me my purse, Mary, there are some gold pieces in it . . .

MARY. But Miss Matty . . . you can't . . .

MISS MATTY. Thank you, dear, please do not interrupt me . . . I know what I am doing. (*She counts out the five sovereigns into* JEM's *hand.*) There, Jem . . . that's gold . . . you can buy Martha's ring tomorrow . . . I apologize on behalf of the Town and County Bank for the inconvenience we have caused you . . .

JEM. Thank you, ma'am . . . I'm sure I hope you won't be the loser . . .

MARTHA. It's very kind of you, ma'am . . . but—

MISS MATTY. Now let Jem out, Martha . . . and lock the door . . . and we will go to bed . . .

MARTHA. But Miss Jenkyns . . . it's your own money you're giving . . .

MISS MATTY. That is quite all right, Martha . . . I shall speak to the director of the bank tomorrow and ask them to put things straight . . . Good night . . .

JEM. Good night, ma'am . . .

(*Exeunt* MARTHA *and* JEM *to kitchen.*)

Miss Pole (*moving* c.). Miss Matty... this is terrible... if the bank has failed, you are ruined...!
Miss Matty. Yes, Miss Pole... I think I am...
Miss Pole (*moving to* Miss M.). Then may I ask if you will think t your duty to offer sovereigns for all the bank notes in Cranford...?
Miss Matty. Dear Miss Pole... it is often very difficult for me to make up my mind about what is right and what is wrong... but when I saw poor Jem standing there before me, I suddenly knew what was my duty... and as for all the other notes in Cranford... I can only wait and see what happens,... and when it does happen, perhaps I shall be helped as I was tonight... to see what is right...
Mary. But Miss Matty...
Miss Matty (*crossing to fire*). And you must understand, dear, that as the Rector's daughter... these poor people look up to me... and to people of our position, and we must not let them down, must we...? Shall we go upstairs...?

(Miss Matty *and* Mary *each take candelabrum and with* Miss P. *in centre move to the stairs very solemnly*...)

And perhaps we shall not be frightened of imaginary robbers, now that we have something more serious to think about...

CURTAIN.

ACT THREE

SET. *The same.*

TIME. *Two days later: a bright sunny morning.*

(*At* RISE: *The stage appears to be deserted but we can hear the noise of very energetic scrubbing and, almost at once, we see the posterior portion of* MARTHA. *She is on her hands and knees scrubbing the front hall for dear life. She backs into view... gives a last wipe to the floor... stands up, dries her hands on her apron, lifts her bucket from the hallway into the parlour and, as she turns, enter* MISS MATTY... *down stairs. She is dressed for the street in bonnet and cape and she carries in her hand an open letter.*)

MARTHA. If you're going out now, ma'am, will you just tell me what you fancy for lunch, before you go...?

MISS MATTY (*who has been thinking about something else*). Oh ... let me see... Something very plain... a mutton chop perhaps... that will be enough for Miss Mary and me... I think...

MARTHA. And for pudding?

MISS MATTY. I don't think we will have any pudding today, Martha...

MARTHA. No pudding...? That's the first time I've heard you say "no pudding"...

MISS MATTY (*breaking* R.). I have no great fancy for sweet things, today. And Martha, I am afraid... you see... that is owing to circumstances, I fear, Martha, that I must give you notice to leave me...

MARTHA (*in violent astonishment*). Leave you...!

MISS MATTY. At the end of the month...

MARTHA. You mean that letter... it says you haven't got no more money...? I didn't like the look of it when I brought it up...

MISS MATTY (*moving* C.). Yes, Martha... it means I am quite ruined... it means I shall have just five shillings a week to live upon... All day yesterday I hoped that perhaps the directors of the bank had made a mistake... But... this letter is quite definite, so you see you must go...

MARTHA. Well, I'm not going, so there...!

MISS MATTY. But, Martha...

MARTHA. Don't "but Martha" me...

MISS MATTY. You must listen to reason...

MARTHA. I'll not listen to reason. Reason always means what someone else has got to say. I've money in the Savings Bank, and I've a good stock of clothes, and I'm not going to leave you, Miss MATTY... not if you gives me notice every hour of the day... (*She puts her arms akimbo in defiance.*)

MISS MATTY. Of course, you would be a great loss to me, Martha...

MARTHA. That I would...

MISS MATTY. And I don't know what I shall do without you...

MARTHA. No more do I... So now where have we got to...?

(MISS MATTY *makes a little, helpless gesture with her hands and turns away... She is a little tearful...*)

You give Jem that five pun, didn't you? When you couldn't afford to... and I 'appens to know you was saving it for this year's dress... And we didn't ought to have took it... But anyways... I'm *not* leaving you.

MISS MATTY. Dear Martha! Do you not understand that I shall not have enough money to support *myself*...let alone ...

(*Enter* MARY *down stairs to* C.)

MARTHA. Money! What's money? I'm surprised you can stand there, Miss Matty, and accuse me of being one to serve Mammon...

MISS MATTY (*turning to* MARY). Mary, you must explain to Martha... about... about leaving me. I am just going out... I shall be gone about an hour...

MARY. Would you not like me to come with you, Miss Matty?

MISS MATTY. No thank you dear... I am going to pay my

debts... I must get them off my conscience... and I have just enough money left to clear everything...
MARY. Debts?
MISS MATTY. Yes, dear... there is five shillings owing at the butcher's from last week... and three and sixpence at the grocer's... and then the rent... (*She pauses with one hand on door.*) You will not mind, Mary, if we have no pudding today...?
MARY. Of course not, Miss Matty...
MISS MATTY (*crossing to door*). Very well, dear... I shall be back in time for lunch...

(*Exit* MISS MATTY. MARY *turns to* MARTHA.)

MARTHA. It's no use telling me I've got to leave... so you can save your breath, Miss Mary...
MARY (*taking* MARTHA *downstage* C.). You see, Martha, it's like this. Miss Matty will have so very little money left... so very little... that, apart from wages, I do not see how she could find you food... she will even be pressed for her own...
MARTHA (*very earnestly*). Was that the reason she wouldn't order a pudding today...?
MARY. Yes, Martha...
MARTHA (*cheering up at the prospect of something to be accomplished*). Then don't you tell her, mind, but I'll make her a pudding, and a pudding she'll like, too, and I'll pay for every bit of it myself, so mind you see she eats it...
MARY. That is very kind of you, Martha...
MARTHA. There's many a one has been comforted in their sorrow by seeing a good pudding...

(*She is bustling off to the kitchen when the doorbell rings. She turns and hastens to the window.*)

Lord! It's the half of Cranford on the doorstep...
MARY (*looking out of the window too*). I'll talk to them, Martha ... you get on with your pudding...

(MARY *opens the door*... MARTHA *goes out to kitchen. Enter* MISS POLE.)

MISS POLE (*in a solemn, important tone*). Is Miss Jenkyns in, Mary..?

MARY. No, Miss Pole... she went out...

MISS POLE. It's as well. I have the honour to head a deputation of Miss Jenkyns' friends... we would like to speak to you...

MARY (*looking very puzzled*). Please come in...

MISS POLE (*looking back over her shoulder*). This way, if you please...

(*And into the room file* MISS BARKER, MRS. FORRESTER, *and* MR. *and* MRS. HOGGINS... *Their faces are all extremely solemn*... *They nod without speaking to* MARY... *and there is over all an air of lugubrious mystery. They come to a halt and stand silently in a bunch.*)

And, now Mary... if I might trouble you for the card table...

(MARY, *in silent amazement, brings the card table forward*... MISS POLE *arranges the chairs to face it*... *almost like pews*... *She sets one chair at the table.*)

If you will be kind enough to be seated, ladies and gentleman...

(*They each take a chair and assume a listening attitude. Meanwhile* MISS POLE *produces from her bag five pieces of paper, five pencils and five envelopes which she hands around. Then she assumes the place at the table*... *looks around*... *blows her nose, clears her throat*... *glances at a small piece of paper concealed in her hand on which are obviously notes, and begins.*)

MISS POLE. First of all I will call upon Miss Smith... that is you, my dear, to confirm the sad report that we have all heard, namely, that Miss Matilda Jenkyns...

MISS B. Our friend of many years standing...

MISS POLE (*glancing at her notes*). Miss Matilda Jenkyns, our dear friend of many years' standing... that is—(*She abandons her speech for a moment.*) My dear Mary, has Miss Matty indeed lost all her fortune...?

MARY. Yes, Miss Pole, I am afraid she has lost everything...

MRS. F. (*beginning to cry*). Oh... the poor soul... the poor sweet soul...

MRS. H. There, there, Mrs. Forrester... we are here to try

and help her...

MISS B. To think that I should live to see the day when a Jenkyns would be in want...

MR. H. A bad business... a very bad business...

(MISS POLE *raps peremptorily on the table for order... They fall silent again.*)

MISS POLE. Thank you, Miss Smith. (MARY *sits* L. C.) I have conversed in private... I made it my business to do so yesterday afternoon... with these friends about the misfortune that has befallen Miss Matilda Jenkyns... and one and all of us have agreed that while we have a superfluity, it is not only a duty, but a pleasure to give what we can to assist her (*She chokes a little.*)

MRS. H. A *true* pleasure...

MR. H. Hear, hear!

MISS POLE (*rapping for order again*). Only in consideration of the feelings of delicate independence existing in the mind of every refined female... we wish to contribute our mites in a secret and concealed manner, so as not to hurt the feelings I have referred to...

MRS. F. (*breaking in*). You see, Mary, that I... that some of us are... no, not exactly poor... but we are not what you may call rich... and we thought that if each of us was to write on a piece of sealed paper what we can afford to give ... though of course we all wish for dear Miss Matty's sake, it was more... (*She straggles off.*)

MR. H. (*rising and moving* C. *to* R. *of table*). The idea, Miss Mary, is for each person here present to write down the annual sum he or she can afford to spare... and that the sealed papers should be handed to Miss Jenkyns' lawyer... so that he can deal with them as he wishes...

MISS POLE (*referring to her notes again*). Thank you, Mr. Hoggins. (HOGGINS *moves above sofa.*) And our object in convening this meeting was to state this resolution of the here assembled citizens of Cranford and to, to... to write down what we can afford to give... Perhaps, you, Miss Smith, would care to say a few words...?

(MISS POLE *sits down suddenly and blows her nose again.*

MARY *rises uncertainly*.)
MARY. I can only say that ... that Miss Matty will be very grateful ... but ... but she is also very proud and I do not know if she will accept your offer ...

MRS. H. Since Miss Matty is not present this morning, she need never hear of this meeting. If Miss Mary, here, could take those papers to Miss Matty's lawyer ... perhaps he could think of some way in which our contribution could be represented as her legal due ...

MISS B. Oh yes, that would be much better ... much better ...

(*They all murmur agreement*.)

MISS POLE. I think we may all thank Mrs. Hoggins for a very excellent suggestion. And now ... ladies and gentlemen ... if you will each take a piece of paper and a pencil ...

(*Each person writes on the piece of paper and seals it carefully* ... HOGGINS *collects them and hands them to* MARY.)

MARY (*rising*). How good of you all ... I wish I could express ...

(*She breaks down and produces a handkerchief* ... *so do all the other ladies*.)

MR. H. (*clearing his throat*). Er—Miss Pole ... !

MISS POLE (*pulling herself together*). Oh yes, Mr. Hoggins has a suggestion to make, Mary ...

(*She raps the table for order and* MR. HOGGINS *rises*.)

(*Formally*.) Ladies! Mr. Hoggins.

MR. H. (*not so formally*). It's like this, Miss Mary, we've been thinking, Mrs. Hoggins and I, that even when all our bits of paper are added up together it isn't going to be such a monstrous big sum of money. No more, maybe, than will pay Miss Matty's rent ... and we wondered what she was going to live on. And we came to the conclusion that, if Miss Matty wouldn't object to it, she might very well become an agent to the East India Tea Company ...

MISS B. Oh dear ... I wish Mrs. Jamieson were here ... perhaps she would not consider it genteel to suggest that that Miss Matty should keep a shop ...

MARY. A shop?
MR. H. Well ... no shop window would be required ... and we thought tea is a good thing to handle ... not greasy or sticky ...
MRS. F. And with a very pleasant odour ...
MISS POLE. Always supposing, of course, that Miss Matty would not feel it a degradation to descend to anything like trade ...
MARY. I do not think Miss Matty would consider it a degradation to earn an honest living ...
MRS. H. Well said, Miss Mary ... And I'm told there is a verra decent living to be made out of tea ...
MISS B. But what would Mrs. Jamieson think of such a thing?
MISS POLE (*rising*). Mrs. Jamieson returned to Cranford yesterday afternoon from Cheltenham. I took the liberty, ladies, of approaching her yesterday evening, and she has promised to give the matter her serious consideration ...
MRS. F. Then if she is returned home, I am surprised not to see her here this morning ...
MISS POLE (*very embarrassed*). Naturally, Mrs. Jamieson wished to be present this morning ... but she ... she has received a shock of a private nature ... a family matter, you understand ...
MRS. H. (*rising and taking her husband's arm*). Miss Pole means, ladies, that my sister-in-law refuses to meet me and Mr. Hoggins here. She's a haughty woman and more addicted to titles than I am so she canna forgive me for getting married again ... That is what ye'd be meaning, is it not, Miss Pole?
MISS POLE. As a matter of fact, she did mention that she would call after ... after ...
MRS. H. (*entirely without rancour*). After we'd taken our leave, no doubt? Well, ladies, we have said what we came to say and will be going in a minute. We're right sorry to be the cause of a rift in your society, but I'd like to tell ye I'm verra proud to be wedded to Mr. Hoggins for ye'll not deny he's an elegant made man and a taking one, and with a guid kind

heart, and what more would a body like me be asking?
MR. H. (*patting her hand*). Thank you, ma'am. (*He turns to the assembly.*) And if Miss Matty should consider the tea trade I will be very happy to communicate with the East India Company for her and give her the best of my advice on the subject...
MARY (*rising*). Thank you very much, Mr. Hoggins... I think your idea about tea is excessively good...
MR. H. Then good morning to you, ladies...
MRS. H. (*as they move to the door*). And give poor Miss Matty my love and tell her not to fash herself for she has naught but friends in Cranford...
   (MR. *and* MRS. HOGGINS *go out.*)
MISS POLE (*rising and rapping the table again*). Ladies, I think we may now bring our meeting to an end...
MRS. F. Poor Mrs. Hoggins... I fear she will be considered a social outcast...
MISS B. I was afraid Mrs. Jamieson might see it in this light...
MISS POLE (*rapping very hard*). We are not assembled, ladies, to discuss Mrs. Hoggins and Mrs. Jamieson... I was about to say that—(*She glances again at the notes.*) that we, the ladies... and one gentleman now departed... of Cranford, in this room assembled, have resolved upon aiding our dear friend, Miss Matilda Jenkyns, to the best of our ability. To this resolution we would like to add that it is our earnest wish that Miss Matty may never learn that we have in any way aided her... or that she is under any obligation to us...
MRS. F. She means it must be a secret, Mary... Just tell the lawyer about it and ask him to give her the money as if it were her own income...
MISS POLE. Thank *you*, Mrs. Forrester. Then I think I may declare the meeting closed...
   (*They all rise and* MISS POLE *collects the pencils and puts them back in her bag.*)
MRS. F. Just say we called, Mary... and *left* our love...
   (*The doorbell rings...* MARY *goes to open it.*)
MISS POLE. That must be Mrs. Jamieson...

Miss B. Oh dear...
Miss Pole. Remember, ladies, no mention of Mrs. Hoggins.
Mrs. F. Certainly not...
Miss B. Not for the world...!
Mrs. J. (*off*). Good morning, Mary... (*Entering.*) Good morning, ladies...
(Mary *follows her* C.)
Miss B. (*unctuously as ever*). Good morning, Mrs. Jamieson, I hope we see you well, and that your sojourn in Cheltenham was of benefit to your health...?
Mrs. J. I found Cheltenham very pleasant... and I think I may say that I am in good health...
Miss B. I am most gratified to hear it, ma'am...
Mary. Pray sit down, Mrs. Jamieson...
Mrs. J. (*enthroning herself at chair* C. *above table* C.). Thank you. (*All sit.*) I may add, ladies, that I am deeply surprised and shocked at the news I have received since my return to Cranford. It should not have been permitted to happen...
Mrs. F. But they did it in London, ma'am... they were already married when they came back to Cranford...
Mrs. J. (*withering her with a frightful glare*). I refer, madam, to the sad condition of Miss Matilda Jenkyns...
Mrs. F. (*flustered*). Oh... I thought you meant Mr. Hoggins.
Mrs. J. Hoggins was a name for which I never cared. It is now a name which I have *forgotten*... you comprehend me?
Mrs. F. Oh yes, ma'am... I'm truly sorry... I...
Mrs. J. The subject is closed.
Miss Pole. I have acquainted these ladies, ma'am, with the suggestion that Miss Matty might consider being an agent for the East India Tea Company.
Miss B. But I am sure, ma'am, that Miss Jenkyns would not dream of opening a shop without first consulting you, as the leader of society, upon the propriety of such a move...
Mrs. J. I promised Miss Pole I would consider the matter, and accordingly I am now come to give you my decision.
Miss Pole. You understand, of course, that a shop window would not be necessary...

MRS. J. Naturally. I have decided, ladies, that in general ... persons who engage in the trade automatically forfeit their right to the privileges of society ...

MARY. But, Mrs. Jamieson ... poor Miss Matty has to live ...

MRS. J. I am aware of that, child, and taking the fact into account, I have decided that, whereas a *married* woman takes the rank of her husband by the strict laws of precedence ... an *unmarried* lady retains the station her father occupied ... *whatever* she may do.

MISS B. Then Miss Matty would not forfeit her position in our society ...

MRS. J. (*with the air of bestowing a great honour*). I have decided that should Miss Jenkyns wish to engage in the tea trade ... she may still be visited with perfect propriety ...

MISS POLE (*with the barest shade of sarcasm*). We are relieved to hear that, ma'am ...

MARY (*smiling*). Very relieved ... !

MISS POLE. And since you signified your wish to contribute to our little fund, ma'am, I have reserved a piece of paper and a pencil for you ...
  (*She produces them ... but* MRS. JAMIESON *rises and moves towards the door.*)

MRS. J. (*producing a folded paper, on which can be seen a small black mark*). That will not be necessary ... I have already written down the sum I am prepared to donate ... It is here ...
  (*She holds out the paper.* MARY *has opened the door for her.*)

MISS POLE. It was most particularly arranged, ma'am, that we should each use an identical piece of paper ... and that we should not sign them ... in that way we can remain *anonymous* ...

MRS. J. I have not signed the paper ... that is merely the Jamieson *crest* ... ! Good morning, ladies.
  (*Exit* MRS. JAMIESON *with a fine sweep.*)

MISS POLE. Her *crest* indeed ... ! I wonder she does not have her coat of arms inscribed on her bonnet ... ! And that remark about a married woman taking the rank of her

husband... that was a slap at Mrs. Hoggins. Well, I for one, shall visit Mrs. Hoggins just whenever I like...
MRS. F. (*rising*). And so shall I... in fact I shall call on her this very afternoon...
MISS POLE. We will go together... And you, Miss Barker...? Will you join us...?
MISS B. (*rising*). You mean you will *defy* the Honourable Mrs. Jamieson...!
MISS POLE (*from the front door where they are ready to go*). Certainly... it is high time somebody did...
MISS B. (*making the decision of her life*). Very well... I will come with you... But I never thought to see this day... never... it's like a revolution...
(*Exit* MISS BARKER.)
MRS. F. Oh dear... a revolution... in *Cranford*...
(*Exit* MRS. FORRESTER.)
MISS POLE (*giving* MARY *a farewell peck*). The French had one. Why shouldn't we...?
(*Exit* MISS POLE.)
(MARY *closes door and comes downstage, smiling and humming* The Marseillaise... MARY *crosses to the kitchen door and calls* MARTHA...)
MARY. Martha... The company has left. You can lay the table for lunch.
(MARY *moves to window. Enter* MARTHA *with tray on which is a cloth, knives, forks, glasses, etc.*)
MARTHA. I thought they'd never go...
MARY. Miss Matty has very good friends, Martha...
MARTHA (*laying the table*). But do you think she would care for this tea-selling business?
MARY. Were you listening, Martha...
MARTHA. You don't think I was a going to let them decide things about Miss Matty without me approving...?
MARY (*laughing*). It seems quite a good idea to me...
MARTHA. So long as I'm here to help her... maybe...
(*The kitchen door opens and* MISS MATTY *peeps in...*)
MISS MATTY. Are they gone...?
MARY. Yes, come in, Miss Matty...

(*Enter* MISS MATTY *from kitchen.*)

MISS MATTY. I saw Mrs. Jamieson's carriage at the front ... Somehow I didn't feel quite up to talking ...

MARTHA (*treating her like a child*). There now ... don't fret. They're gone, so give me your bonnet and put your feet up ...

MARY. And Mr. and Mrs. Hoggins came too ... and they have an idea ... a very practical idea, I think; they suggested that you might perhaps become an agent for the East India Tea Company ...

MISS MATTY. An agent?

MARTHA (*passing her across*). She means have a little shop and sell tea ... Now, your mutton chop is ready ... so sit up to the table ...

(*Exit* MARTHA *to kitchen.*)

MISS MATTY (*alarmed*). A shop ... ! To *sell* tea ... Oh dear, I'm afraid I could not do that ...

MARY. Mrs. Jamieson gave it as her opinion that you would not lose your social position by engaging in trade ...

MISS MATTY. My dear Mary ... I had not even thought about social position ... but a *shop*!

MARY. You would not need a shop-window, Miss Matty ... it could be more like an office ...

MISS MATTY. You misunderstand me, dear ... It is just that *men* go into shops ... and I do not think I could serve a gentleman ... for they have such loud sharp ways with them ... and they count their *change* so quickly ... and although I have tried all my life ... I still cannot count up change ...

MARY (*smiling*). But it is their wives who do the household shopping ... I think you would find all your customers ladies ...

(*Enter* MARTHA *with the mutton chop.*)

MISS MATTY. Oh dear! Have you not explained to her, Mary ...

MARTHA (*in a motherly manner*). She's explained all right. There now ... you eat up your nice chop ... it'll warm your vitals ...

(MARTHA *adjusts a cushion at* MISS MATTY's *back*.)

MISS MATTY. Thank you, Martha... But you *must* understand that I am in reduced circumstances... I cannot afford the luxury of a servant...

MARTHA. Then if that's the way it is... you'll just have to take orders from me... so eat your dinner for there's someone a waiting to talk to you out in the kitchen...

MISS MATTY. Who, Martha? We must not keep anyone waiting in the kitchen...

MARTHA. If I bring him in... will you go on eating?

MISS MATTY. Yes... yes, indeed I will...

MARY. Bring him in, Martha...

MARTHA. All right... But he's a bit difficult...

(*Exit* MARTHA. *The ladies commence to eat. Suddenly from the kitchen comes the noise of scuffling and clumping and hoarse whispering...* MISS MATTY *and* MARY *look up in some alarm. The door opens and shuts again as by some invisible agency, but after a little while* MARTHA *enters dragging after her a red-faced* JEM. *He is covered with confusion and finds his only relief in perpetually sleeking down his hair.*)

MARTHA (*panting for breath*). Please, ma'am... it's Jem Hearn again. (*She pauses but* JEM *says nothing*.) Go on, you great oaf... tell her...!

JEM. It's like this, ma'am... you see Martha, here...

(*But he cannot continue and falls to sleeking his hair again.*)

MARTHA (*taking over, but still breathless*). You see, ma'am... Jem wants to marry me offhand... right away without waiting... And please, ma'am... we want to take a lodger... just one quiet lodger to make our two ends meet ... and we'd take any house comfortable; and, oh, Miss Matty, if I may be so bold, would you have any objection to lodging with us? Jem wants it as much as I do... (*To* JEM.) Go on, you big oaf...! Why can't you back me? (*To* MISS MATTY.) He's dazed at being called on to speak before quality... But he does want it all the same, very bad... don't you, Jem?

JEM (*moving* C.). It's like this, ma'am... Martha's taken me all of a sudden... and such quick work does flabbergast a man.

MARTHA. Don't mind him, ma'am, he'll come to...

JEM. It's not that I'm against it, ma'am... only Martha has such quick ways with her when once she takes a thing into her head; and marriage, ma'am, marriage nails a man, as one may say...

(MARTHA *gives him such a nudge as almost to unbalance him.*)

MARTHA. 'Twas only last night he was an-axing me and an-axing me... and now he's only taken aback with the suddenness of the joy... (*She gives him another great nudge.*)

JEM. I dare say I shan't mind if after it's once over...

MARTHA. And Jem, you are just as full as me about wanting a lodger... (*A nudge.*) You see we'd have to have a lodger to make the ends meet...

JEM. Ay! If Miss Matty would lodge with us... otherwise I've no mind to be cumbered with strange folk in the house...

(*This enrages* MARTHA *who gives him another poke with her elbow.*)

MISS MATTY. Marriage is a very solemn thing...

JEM (*eagerly*). It is, *indeed*, ma'am... (*He gets another jolt.*) Not that I've no objections to Martha...

MARTHA (*getting very red in the face*). I like that, Jem Hearn... shaming me before my missus and all...

JEM. Nay, now! Martha, don't ee! Don't ee! Only a man likes to have breathing time...

(*He tries to take her hand, but she is really offended... and bounces out of the room. Exit* MARTHA.)

MARY. I think it is a wonderful plan, Jem... and I am sure Martha will make you a very good wife...

JEM. Ay... I always looked on her as to be my wife... sometime; and she has often and often spoke of you as the kindest lady that ever was, Miss Matty, and though the plain truth is, I would not like to be troubled with lodgers of the common run, yet if, ma'am, you'd honour us by living with us, I'm sure Martha would do her best to make you comfortable.

MISS MATTY (*rather near tears*). I'm sure she would, Jem... I'm sure she would...

JEM. And I'd keep out of your way as much as I could, which I reckon would be the best kindness such an awkward chap as me could do.

(MARTHA's *head appears round kitchen door.*)

MARTHA. Go on... ask her about the house... you big fool...

(MARTHA's *head is withdrawn.*)

JEM. Well... we was a thinking... me and Martha, that is, Martha and me... we was thinking that as there isn't a house vacant hereabouts... and if Miss Matty here is going to give up this one... Well, if it'd be comfortable... we might take this one and Miss Matty could keep on in her own rooms seeing as how we'd only be needing one... one bedroom, and the kitchen...

MISS MATTY (*all but crying*). Jem... I... I cannot... I cannot... tell you how... how...

MARY. I think it is a perfect idea...

JEM (*backing awkwardly to the door but unable to make an exit*). And I hope you'll excuse me, ma'am... for being a bit awkward, but I'm sure I mean kindly... and I'm a bit fluttered by being pushed straight ahead into matrimony... and I mayn't express myself conformable... but I, well... I...

MISS MATTY (*equally at a loss for words*). Oh, Jem... I... wish... I...

(*The conversation has reached a complete deadlock and* JEM *has backed up against the door where he stands mopping his forehead as if he had completed a day's work. Suddenly we hear* MARTHA's *voice off.*)

MARTHA. Come along out, you great oaf... you've said all you've got to say...

(*And with this, her brawny arm appears, takes his sleeve, and yanks him headlong into the kitchen. Exit* JEM. *Sounds of scuffling and buffetting follow his exit...*)

Miss Matty (*pushing aside her plate*). Oh, Mary dear... and to think that for ever so long I refused to let Martha have a follower...!

Mary. Can you not eat any more, Miss Matty...?

Miss Matty. How can I eat when everyone is so kind...?

Mary. I think Martha has been preparing a special pudding for you...

Miss Matty. But I didn't order one...

Mary. But this has been paid for out of her own purse... I am afraid we shall offend her if you do not eat it.

Miss Matty. Then I will eat it, dear, if it chokes me...

Mary. Remember... it is to be a great surprise!

(*Enter* Martha *bearing aloft a platter on which is a magnificent gelatine pudding made in the representation of a lion couchant! It is a bright pink colour and has currants for eyes. She places it before* Miss Matty, *beaming triumphantly.*)

Martha. There!

Miss Matty. How beautiful...! How...

(*But she is too much affected to speak, so she rises and shakes* Martha *warmly by the hand...*)

I should like to keep it for *ever* under a glass shade...!

Martha. Now you eat it up... every bit of it... the eyes is currants... so they're wholesome too.

Miss Matty (*wiping her eyes with her handkerchief*). Martha! I should like to tell you... it was the *luckiest* day of my life, when I lost my money...

(*At this,* Martha *puts her handkerchief to her face and bolts out of the room.*)

(*Seating herself again.*) Do you remember, dear... in the Bible... when the Children of Israel were hungry...?

Mary (*puzzled*). Yes, Miss Matty...?

Miss Matty. I was just thinking, dear... that *manna* must have looked like this!

(*The lights begin to fade. The gauze drops and* Mrs. Gaskell *enters* D.L. *in front of the gauze and speaks to the audience as* Mary *and* Miss Matty *sit silently over their pudding.*)

MRS. GASKELL. I shall never forget that wonderful pudding! And never was there a pudding so difficult to eat, every morsel seemed to choke us ... our hearts were so full. How long ago it seems ... but even now I almost imagine I can taste it ...

(*There is now a* COMPLETE BLACKOUT *behind* MRS. GASKELL *who sighs and continues.*)

Well, now you have seen all the ingredients of our revolution. The aristocracy, as represented by Lady Glenmire, has descended to a union with a mere commoner, a middle-class commoner with the name of Hoggins to boot. A very shocking fall! And as for the masses, for the poor underdog, for poor Jem Hearn ... you have seen how he came up ... and how very pleased we were to see him.

(*Lights behind the gauze go slowly up and reveal the same set, but with certain radical changes. Just inside the door of* MISS MATTY'S *parlour is a counter on which is stacked a row of canisters containing tea. They are labelled Gongou, Souchong, Pekoe, Gunpowder, etc., in large gold letters. There is a pair of scales and other evidences of trade. The front door stands open, for it is a summer morning. Leading from the door to the counter is a pathway of carpet ... two chairs are placed by the counter for the convenience of customers.* MISS MATTY *sits behind the counter; she is wearing an apron over the same morning dress that we know ... and her cap is a little plainer than of yore. Behind* MISS MATTY *is affixed to the wall a small sign: "Miss Matilda Jenkyns, Licensed to sell Tea".*

On the counter, as well as the canisters are a small basket of eggs, a basket of strawberries, and one or two glass jars containing summer flowers. It is rather like "teacher's desk". There is also a huge glass jar with a stopper in which are sponge fingers. The whole room is flooded with sunlight and warmth.)

MRS. GASKELL (*continues*). I wonder if Miss Matty still thinks she was lucky to lose her money! Things have changed considerably in the last months, as you can see ... ! This was the day on which I paid my first visit to Miss Matty

ACT III] CRANFORD 97

since the opening of the shop. It was Martha who wrote to me this time ... a very strange letter a little difficult to decipher ... but she begged me very urgently to come ... so come I did, hardly stopping to pack my bag ... and very curious indeed as to what could need my attention so urgently in Cranford ...

(*Exit* MRS. GASKELL.)

(*Enter* MISS BARKER *at front door. She carries a silk parasol which she closes as she enters. On her arm is her shopping basket.*)

MISS B. (*very brightly*). Good morning, Miss Matty ... what a lovely day!

MISS MATTY (*looking up from her crochet*). Why, Miss Barker ... good morning. It is beautiful is it not .... ?

MISS B. Has the new Pekoe come in yet ... ?

MISS MATTY (*patting the canister*). Yes, indeed, last evening.

MISS B. Then a quarter of a pound, please ...

(MISS MATTY *opens the canister and prepares to serve the tea—then pauses.*)

MISS MATTY. I have not tasted it yet ... but if you could call again in about twenty minutes I could brew a pot and we might try it ...

(*Enter* JEM *from kitchen* ... *He crosses to front door.*)

JEM. Mornin', Miss Barker ...

MISS B. Good morning, Jem ... How is Martha ... ?

JEM (*starting to polish the sign on the door*). She's well enough, thank you, ma'am ... leastways as well as you might expect ... (*He is gazing up the street.*)

MISS B. (*moving* C.). And why are you not at work this morning, Jem ... ?

MISS MATTY. He has a holiday today ... But Jem! That is the third time this morning you have polished that sign ...

JEM (*slightly confused*). Is that so, ma'am ... well now ...

(*He takes a last look up the street and returns towards the kitchen.*)

MISS MATTY. And would you please ask Martha to put the kettle on ...

JEM (*very vague and preoccupied*). Yes, ma'am ... the kettle ... Kettle o' water, ma'am ... ?

Miss Matty. Of course, Jem... to make tea... Boiling water...

Jem. Yes, ma'am... boiling water...
     (*Exit* Jem *to kitchen.*)

Miss Matty. I cannot think what has come over Jem these last few weeks. He seems so strange and pre-occupied...

Miss B. Well, I'll just run down to Johnson's and call in later for the tea... Oh, I forgot... I picked these for you from my garden... red currants—
    (*She produces from her basket a pottery basin of red currants.*)

Miss Matty. Oh, Miss Barker...! How good of you...!
    (*They are placed with the other offerings on the counter.*)

Miss B. (*moving to door*). Have to pick them... before the birds get at them...
    (*She is half way out of the door when she pops her head back in...*)
By the way... I just heard from Mrs. Deacon at the Coach and Horses... Mrs. Jamieson's got the gout...

Miss Matty. Poor woman! Badly?

Miss B. (*telegraphically*). Severe pain... big toe... left foot...
     (*Exit* Miss Barker.)
    (Miss Matty *shakes her head sympathetically and resumes her crochet work. As she works she starts to sing softly to herself.*
    Miss Matty *is so busy with her work that she does not notice when* Mary *enters. She peeps round the door and then softly tiptoes to the counter. She is wearing a summer dress, and a straw hat... she carries her own bag...*)

Mary. A pound of Pekoe, please, Miss Jenkyns...

Miss Matty (*starting up, at first to serve a customer... then seeing who it is*). Why, Mary...!
    (Mary, *dropping her bag, runs* D.S. *below counter. They embrace.*)

Mary. Miss Matty...!

Miss Matty (*not waiting for answers*). But why did you not warn me that you were coming, my dear...? How pretty you look ... and how delightful to see you ... Is Matthew bringing your bag? Did you come from the station in the fly?

MARY. Yes. I came in the fly ... but my bag is so small I carried it myself ...

MISS MATTY. Then excuse me one minute, dear ... Matthew's wife has had another of her attacks ... I want to send her these eggs ... I will not be a minute ...

(*She seizes the eggs from the counter and runs out of the front door calling.*)

Matthew ... ! Matthew ... !

(*Enter* MARTHA *from kitchen.*)

MARY (*moving* C.). Here I am, Martha ... I came as soon as I got your letter ... Is anything wrong?

MARTHA (*moving* C.). Thank you, Miss Mary, for coming so quick ... it's good to see you again too .. I'm not much of a one for the writing of letters, and Jem said as how you wouldn't mind ... and you see, we couldn't ask Miss Matty ...

MARY. But what is it, Martha? Tell me.

MARTHA. Well, miss, it's like this ... we talked it over, Jem and me ... and we decided as how it was his place to tell you ... seeing as how it's just as much his fault as it is mine ... and being more conformable coming from him ... (*She looks out of the window.*) Here she is ... a coming back (MARY *breaks* L.) ... Shhh ... ! I'll take her upstairs and Jem'll have a word with you ... he took the day off special ...

(*Enter* MISS MATTY.)

MISS MATTY. Is not this a delightful surprise, Martha? ... to see Miss Mary so unexpectedly?

MARTHA. It is that. Now, Miss Matty ... I was thinking we'll have to get her room ready for her ... and if you wouldn't mind just a'coming up the stairs along of me ...

MISS MATTY. Yes ... oh yes, of course ...

MARTHA. That's the way, then ... and Miss Mary'll keep an eye on the shop ...

(*She gives a conspiratorial glance at* MARY.)

MISS MATTY. Thank you, Mary...
MARTHA (*like a mother-hen*).   Come along of you, then...
(*They go up stairs.* MARTHA *pointing meaningly at the kitchen door. When they are out of sight,* MARY, *looking very baffled, opens the kitchen door and calls.*)
MARY. Jem...!
(*Enter* JEM.)
JEM. Ah... Miss Mary! I been keeping a look out for you. Thought I might get a chance for a word with you afore... afore...
MARY. It's all right, Jem... Martha has taken her upstairs...
JEM (*in great confusion, as usual*). Well then, ma'am... it's like this. Martha and me... we're real worried on account of Miss Matty... and Martha says she won't approve of it at all... and she might be wanting to move ... and she says it'll give her a monstrous big shock anyways...
MARY. But Jem!... Tell me... what has *happened*...?
JEM. Well... it hasn't happened yet, miss... in a manner of speaking, that is...
MARY. Then tell me, Jem, and I am sure I shall be able to prevent it.
JEM (*mopping his forehead*). On no, you won't, miss... (*Then with a rush.*)   On account of it's a BABY...!
MARY. A baby...?
JEM. Yes, miss... Martha and me... we're expectin'...
MARY. But, Jem, that is splendid news... I must congratulate you... (*They shake hands.*)   But why are you afraid to tell Miss Matty...?
JEM. Well, miss... you see... I don't think she rightly understands about such things... and having a baby... well, Martha, says she won't think it's proper...
MARY (*laughing*). But I am sure she will be very pleased...
JEM. We did try to tell her, miss... we said as how we was expecting an addition to the family... and she said "Indeed" she said... and "Where from?"... and then we give it up.
MARY. Leave it to me, Jem... I will explain to her... When is the baby due?

JEM. Not till September, miss... But break it gentle...
MARY. I will, Jem...
  (*Enter* MISS MATTY *and* MARTHA *downstairs.* JEM *goes out hurriedly.*)
MISS MATTY. The bed is very well aired, Mary... it's the same room, we always keep it ready for you...
MARY. Thank you, Miss Matty. (*To* MARTHA.) Mrs. Hearn... I want to congratulate you... Your husband has just told me...
  (*She kisses* MARTHA.)
MISS MATTY (*in some surprise*). My dear...?
MARTHA (*in a great hurry to leave before the news is broken*). Thank you, miss... But I'm busy... be careful how you tell her...
  (*Exit* MARTHA *quickly to kitchen.*)
MISS MATTY. My dear, how very strange!
MARY (*moving* C.). Miss Matty! Jem and Martha have some news... some very good news...
MISS MATTY. Indeed... This is the first I have heard of it... It couldn't be that relation they are expecting...?
MARY (*smiling*). Yes... a relation... a baby...!
MISS MATTY (*quite casually*). We must get the spare room ready... when...? (*She suddenly stops.*) A baby...! Oh...! Martha's going to have a baby...?
MARY. But not until September...
MISS MATTY. But should she not be in bed...? A doctor...!
MARY. Not for a long time, yet, Miss Matty...
MISS MATTY. You are certain...? You must forgive me, dear... but I have had very little experience with babies...
MARY. They were frightened that you might not approve...
MISS MATTY. Approve...! Oh, Mary...! Do you think she will let me play with it...? I must buy it a ball...
  (*We feel almost she is off to buy the ball right now...*)
MARY. It will be a year or two before it can play with a ball, Miss Matty...
MISS MATTY (*attempting to be very practical*). Of course... how foolish of me. I have been told that they are very small to begin with...

(*Enter* MRS. FORRESTER *at shop door. She is furling her parasol* . . . *her shopping basket is over her arm.*)

MRS. F. Good morning, Miss Matty. A quarter of a pound of Congou, if you please . . .

MISS MATTY. Oh, good morning, Mrs. Forrester . . . Mary will serve you. (*Moving* D.R.) I have to go and congratulate Martha . . .

(*She is running from the room but looks back over her shoulder to call.*)

Why not wait and try the Pekoe? The Congou is *so* expensive . . .

(*Exit* MISS MATTY *to kitchen.*)

MARY. How are you, dear Mrs. Forrester . . . ?

MRS. F. (*moving to counter*). How are you, my dear . . . ? Martha told me you were coming . . . and I see you have broken the news . . .

MARY. You knew about the baby?

MRS. F. My dear Mary, the whole of Cranford has known for weeks . . . only nobody would break the news to Miss Matty . . . How did she take it . . . ?

MARY. She's very happy about it . . . a little bewildered, perhaps . . . And what other news has Cranford to offer? Is Mrs. Jamieson speaking to Mrs. Hoggins, yet . . . ?

MRS. F. Oh, certainly not, my dear . . . have you not heard? It is quite terrible.

MARY. Remember I have not been in Cranford for nearly a year . . .

MRS. F. (*delighted to be first with the gossip*). Well, you see it was like this . . . Mrs. Hoggins issued invitations to a small supper . . . very genteel, of course . . . and Mrs. Jamieson refused very rudely . . . but *we* all went . . . !

MARY (*eagerly*). And then what happened?

MRS. F. I have forgotten exactly . . . but everybody seemed to invite everybody . . . only of course Mrs. Jamieson would never go . . . and at last *she* gave a party and didn't invite Mrs. Hoggins . . . and *we* didn't go . . . !

MARY. How brave of you . . . !

MRS F. And so nobody has seen her for months except when

she goes by in her carriage ... and they say she is monstrous bad-tempered at home and even her servants are giving her notice ...! (*She breaks* C.)
(*Enter* MISS MATTY *with a tray on which are teacups.*)
MISS MATTY. We are just going to try the new Pekoe, Mrs. Forrester ... you must take a cup ...
MRS. F. (*moving to sofa*). But I wanted Congou ...
MISS MATTY (*hardly listening to her*). So expensive. And have you heard about Martha's baby ...?
MRS. F. Mary just told me ... *What* a surprise ...!
MISS MATTY (*taking teapot and opening the canister of Pekoe*). I shall have to take great care of her, of course ...
MRS. F. And have you heard about Mrs. Jamieson ...?
MISS MATTY (*following*). About Mrs. Jamieson?
MRS. F. I've just heard she is laid up with gout ...
MISS MATTY. Poor woman. Badly?
MRS. F. Dreadful pain ... the big toe of the left foot ...
(*Enter* MISS POLE ... *also with shopping basket.*)
MISS POLE. Good morning everybody ... Why ... Mary, here again in Cranford after all these months ...!
MISS MATTY. Miss Pole ... we have the greatest news ...! Martha's going to have a baby ...!
MISS POLE (*who of course knows quite well*). Well! I declare! You could knock me over with a feather ...! When?
MISS MATTY. In September ... (*Moving* D.R.) but it will be very small at first, of course ...
MISS POLE. And speaking of news ... I just happened to run into Mrs. Deacon who tells me Mrs. Jamieson ...
MRS. F. (*very quickly*). Gout ...! Big toe ... left foot ...
MISS POLE (*crestfallen*). The pain, I understand ... is severe ...
MRS. F. So I am told ...
MISS POLE. And I dare say she will now wish she had not fallen out with Mr. Hoggins ...
MARY. You think the gout is retribution ...?
MISS POLE. I think she will need a doctor ... and Mr. Hoggins is the only doctor in Cranford ...!
MRS. F. I never thought of that ...
MISS MATTY. I was about to brew a little of the new Pekoe,

Miss Pole, I hope you will join us in a cup...?
MISS POLE. Thank you... I just dropped in for a quarter of a pound of Gunpowder...
MISS MATTY (*on the way to the kitchen with the tea pot*). Do try the Pekoe first... it is *so* much cheaper... The kettle is on the boil... please be seated, ladies... I will not be a moment.
    (*Exit* MISS MATTY *to kitchen. The ladies come round the counter and seat themselves.*)
MARY. Please tell me... if you all know about Martha's baby... why do you pretend to be so surprised...?
MISS POLE (*sitting above counter*). Well, dear, you see since Miss Matty started the shop, we all drop in and she likes to be able to tell us some news... She would be so disappointed if we already knew about it.
    (*Enter* MISS BARKER.)
MISS B. Good morning, ladies... How are you, Mary, my dear...
MARY. Come and sit down, Miss Barker... and what is *your* news?
MISS B. (*sitting below counter*). Thank you, dear. Well... I just ran into Mrs. Deacon... and she tells me that Mrs. Jamieson...
MISS POLE (*like a machine gun*). Big toe, left foot...
MRS. F. Severe pain...
MISS B. (*very disappointed*). Oh... you already knew...
MARY (*laughing*). Oh, dear... why do I ever leave Cranford...!
    (*Enter* MISS MATTY *with the teapot.*)
MISS MATTY (*moving to behind counter*). Now ladies... tea... the new Pekoe...
    (*Enter at shop door* MRS. HOGGINS *and* MR. HOGGINS.)
MRS. H. Good morning to you, ladies... And here's Mary, bonnier than ever...
MR. H. I see we're in time for a cup of tea, Miss Matty...
MISS MATTY. How very pleasant... please sit down...
MRS. H. (*sits on sofa.* MR. H. *sits beside her*). I have just heard that my poor sister-in-law Mrs. Jamieson has a verra sharp

touch of the gout...
MISS MATTY. Oh... indeed... Poor Mrs. Jamieson...! She must be very lonely these days... I really think I should visit her...
MISS POLE. Don't you dare, Miss Matty! Just wait... if the gout gets bad enough she will have to visit Mr. Hoggins...
MARY. There's a carriage stopping at the gate...
MISS POLE (*in great excitement*). There is only *one* carriage in Cranford...!
MARY. Yes... it is Mrs. Jamieson's...
MISS MATTY. I expect it is her coachman with a note...
MARY. No... she's getting out...
MISS POLE (*jumping up*). She's walking with a stick... she's coming up the path...
(MISS POLE *sits down quickly and composes herself.*)
MISS B. Oh... I feel quite frightened...!
(MISS MATTY *is about to rise but* MISS POLE *restrains her.* HOGGINS *breaks to fireplace.*)
MISS POLE (*sitting, in a hoarse whisper*). Stay there, Miss Matty... *We'll* show her. (*She rises and moves to* L. C.)
MRS. JAMIESON *very slowly heaves into view... she is walking with a stick... but is as haughty as ever.*)
MRS. J. Miss Jenkyns...! Miss Jenkyns...!
(*She raps the counter with her stick.*)
MISS MATTY. Good morning, Mrs. Jamieson... is there something I can do for you?
MRS. J. I will take a pound... of your best Souchong, please, Miss Jenkyns...
MISS MATTY. Souchong... yes...
(*She starts to take the top off the canister... very nervously...* MRS. JAMIESON *turns and sees the company.*)
MRS. J. Oh... I see you have friends...
(*The ladies are all as stiff as pokers but take no notice of her at all.*)
MISS MATTY. Yes, Mrs. Jamieson... old friends... of yours, too...
MRS. J. (*above the counter seating herself so that she does not look directly at them*). I have been troubled a little with gout of

late...
MISS MATTY. The left foot...?
MRS. J. The right...!
MISS POLE (*rising, sotto voce*). That Mrs. Deacon was always unreliable... (*Moving to sit below fire.*)
MISS MATTY. I am sorry to hear that, Mrs. Jamieson. Perhaps you should see a doctor...
MRS. J. I have also been unable to entertain of late owing to trouble with my servants...
MISS MATTY. I *am* sorry. I am so lucky, I feel, not to have servants...
MRS. J. How is it possible to live without servants?... Who is to open the door...?
MISS MATTY. My door is always open...!
MRS. J. How fortunate.
MISS MATTY (*who has finished weighing the tea*). There... a pound... Will that be all...?
MRS. J. (*making no attempt to take it*). I should be glad, Miss Jenkyns, if you would take tea with me some day...
MISS MATTY. I should be most happy, Mrs. Jamieson... Thursday is my early closing day...
MRS. J. Then shall we say next Thursday...?
MISS MATTY. I am afraid my Thursdays are rather taken up... But five weeks from next Thursday, I should be delighted to accept...
MRS. J. (*taken aback*). Oh... I see...
MISS MATTY. But any morning, if you would care to drop in about this time, I shall be very happy to offer you a cup of tea here...
MRS. J. (*clearing her throat and at last beginning to climb down*). I see you are taking tea now... perhaps... er...?
MISS MATTY. Why, certainly... if you would care to meet all my friends...?
    (*There is a long and pregnant pause while* MRS. JAMIESON *fights an inward battle.*)
MRS. J. (*rising majestically*). I will meet your friends, Miss Jenkyns...
MISS MATTY (*rising and moving* C.). Then, first of all... I

should like you to shake hands with Mrs. Hoggins...
MRS. J. (*flinching a little*). How do you do... Mrs. Hoggins?
MRS. H. (*rising and shaking her hand warmly*). I'm verra well, ma'am... and I'm distressed to hear about your gout... my husband, here, will be happy to advise you...
MR. H. (*moving U. C., shaking hands*). I certainly will, ma'am..
(MRS. HOGGINS *sits again.*)
MRS. J. (*still rather coldly*). Thank you, sir... I will remember your offer...
(*She sits R. C.*)
MISS POLE. It is wonderful, is it not, Mrs. Jamieson, what a difference a touch of gout can make to one's outlook upon life...
(*Enter* MARTHA *from D.R.*)
MISS MATTY. Another cup please, Martha.
(*Exit* MARTHA.)
MRS. J. (*she sits on chair C. next to sofa*). I understood you to say, Miss Matty, that you had no servant...?
MISS MATTY. Oh... I have not... Martha is not my servant... she is my landlady...
(*Enter* MARTHA *with cup.*)
...and what is more, she is going to have a baby! Oh! My dear Martha... You ought to be resting... sit down... sit down at once...!
(*And she literally pushes* MARTHA *into the seat beside* MRS. JAMIESON *upon the sofa...*)
MARTHA (*furiously embarrassed*). But, ma'am!
MRS. J. Landlady? I could have sworn this was the servant I have seen here before...!
MISS MATTY (*quite angry for the first time in her life*). Mrs. Jamieson... I asked you to take tea with my friends... This is my very dear friend, Mrs. Jem Hearn... (*There is a long pause and* MISS MATTY *is trembling as she adds.*) I should like to introduce you... Mrs. Hearn... Mrs. Jamieson...!
(*The pause now becomes almost unbearable... as the ladies watch in horror to see what will happen.* MRS. JAMIESON *looks round the room for help but meets the stoniest*

glares . . . at last she slowly puts out her hand.)
Mrs. J. How do you do, madam!
(*The ladies break into delighted conversation.*)

CURTAIN.

Property Plot

Act I. Scene 1

Stage
Newspapers on floor, by window.
Glass vase for chrysants. on window table.
One small well-bound book on table L.
St. James's Chronicle on table L.
Bell rope down stage of fireplace.
Five fire tongs, etc.
Candlesticks with candles. One on window table, one up stage end of fireplace.
Off L.
Mary's bag.
Bunch of chrysants. for MATTY.
Hat in hatbox for MARY.
Off R.
Large silver tray for MARTHA.
Mop and bucket for MARTHA.
CHECK
    Fire   alight
    Candles   out
    Windows closed
    Gauze   down.

Act I. Scene 2

Stage
Set card table and two chairs centre.
Move armchair left against wall down stage of window. Small table upstage of chair.
On card table, cards for "preference", four pencils, four score cards.
Wax tapers and matches on mantelpiece by candles, on small table L.
Move candlestick from window table to small table L.
Off L.
Burke's Peerage. A large brown paper covered book for MISS POLE.
Note for MARTHA on small silver salver.
St. James's Chronicle for MISS POLE.
Off R.
Hand towel for MATTY.
Plate with 8 slices bread and butter for MARTHA.
Plate with 8 sponge fingers for MARTHA.
Set on flat tray following: Lace tray cloth, 8 cups, saucers and spoons, silver tea pot, sugar basin and tongs, plate with slices of lemon. (To be placed on silver tray when brought off stage by MARTHA.)
CHECK
    Silver tray under sofa.
    Windows closed.

Act II. Scene 1

Stage
Furniture returns to Act I, Sc. 1.
On small table L.
    Fashion book.
On top of fashion book
    Small silver tea tray with dirty cup, etc., knife and plate.
On window table
    Polished wooden box containing old bills and under bills bundle of letters tied with ribbon.
    St. James's Chronicle.
Off R.
A single candlestick lit.
CHECK
    Windows closed
    Curtains open
    Fire   alight
    Candles One set ready to light on small table left with matches and wax tapers. (This is lit in cue during the prologue to Act.)
               One set ready with tapers and matches up stage end of mantelpiece.
    Gauze   down.

ACT II. SCENE 2

Stage
Card table set for four as Act 1, Scene 2, but with four chairs.
Purse on window table for MATTY containing two pennies and five sovereigns.

Off R.
Silver tray: on it lace cloth and five cups of tea poured out. Silver sugar basin, tongs and Plate of lemon slices.

Off L.
(In Hall). Military hat for MISS POLE, and capes, etc., for MISS POLE, MRS. FORRESTER and MISS BARKER.

Off L.
Large basket covered with green cloth containing (supposedly) silver for MISS POLE.

Personal
Purse and two pennies, MRS. FORRESTER and MISS BARKER.
£5 note Town and County Bank, for HERN.

CHECK
Windows	closed
Curtains	closed
Fire	alight
Candles	alight.

ACT III

Stage
Furniture returns as Act I, except armchair L. moved three feet L. and small table L. moved to R. side of armchair L.

Off Stairs
Letter for MISS MATTY.

Off L.
Reticule for MISS POLE containing 5 pencils, 5 envelopes and 5 pieces of paper.
Letter with black crest for MRS. JAMIESON.

Off R.
Silver tray: on it tray cloth, 2 serving spoons, 2 knives and forks, 2 dessert spoons and forks, 2 glasses of water, silver cruet, for MARTHA.
Two plates of mutton chops and veg., etc.
Silver platter with pudding.

Off in Hall
Bucket and scrubbing brush for MARTHA.

CHECK
Windows	closed
Curtains	open
Candles	out
Front door	open
Gauze	up.

Scene change—
Counter moved in. (See change plot.)
On it:
Crochet work for MISS MATTY.
4 tea canisters.
4 tea scoops.
Scales and weights.
Paper bags for tea.
Small basket of eggs.
Huge glass jar with sponge fingers.
Linoleum on floor, sign behind counter on wall.

Off L.
Shopping basket containing red currants in basin for MISS BARKER.
Small bag, MARY.
Shopping basket for MRS. FORRESTER.
Shopping basket for MISS POLE.

Off R.
Polishing rag for JEM HERN.
Tray: on it 8 empty tea cups, saucers, spoons, sugar basin and tongs, plate with slices of lemon, tea pot for MISS MATTY.

CHECK
Front door	open
Windows	closed
Fire	out
Curtains	open
Candles	out.